DECORATING IN
BLUE AND
WHITE

DECORATING IN
BLUE AND
WHITE

Lynda Burgess

CASSELL

747

DISCARD

First published in the UK 1996 by
Cassell
Wellington House
125 Strand
London WC2R OBB

First published in paperback in 1997

Distributed in the United States by Sterling Publishing, Co. Inc.
387 Park Avenue South, New York, NY 10016

British Library Cataloguing in Publication Data
A catalogue record for this book is available from the British Library

HBK ISBN 0-304-34635-7
PBK ISBN 0-304-34927-5

Printed and bound in Spain

PHOTOGRAPHIC CREDITS

Photographs supplied by Robert Harding Syndication.
Jacket front: Country Homes and Interiors, except TR Graham Rae/Ideal Home, BL Homes and Gardens; back clockwise left to
right Polly Wreford/Homes and Gardens, Chris Drake/Country Houses and Interiors, Country Houses and Interiors.
Country Homes and Interiors 5T, 5B; Jan Baldwin 8, 34–5, 37T, 48; Nic Barlow 33; Tim Beddow 20; Simon Brown 21B, 102;
Joanne Cowrie 28–9; Chris Drake 10, 59T, 73; Tim Goffe 21T, 95, 99; John Heseltine 90; Kibran Howard 102–3; Tim Imrie 14;
Tom Leighton 61; Mark Lucscombe-Whyte 45B; John Mason 109R; James Merrell 55; Hugh Palmer 70–1, 81; Peter Rauter 80;
Andreas Van Einsiedel 12–13, 41; Fritz Von der Schulenberg 36, 118; Mark Wood 9; Polly Wreford 11, 76, 85T, 108.
Homes and Gardens/Jan Baldwin 28; David Barrett 29T, 60, 126; James Merrell 34, 76–7, 117; Trevor Richards 6, 17T,
18–19, 84, 91, 98, 109L, 113, 122; Andreas Van Einsiedel 64; Polly Wreford 15T, 18, 37B, 69; Jeremy Young 25.
Homes and Ideas/Ian Skelton 59B.
Ideal Home/Dominic Blackmore 17, 84–5, 85B, 94; Les Meeham 6–7; Graham Rae 49T.
Options/Simon Brown 29B; Chris Drake 2, 54–5, 68, 104, 105, 119; Tom Leighton 87; Pia Tryde 1, 70.
Woman and Home/Steve Dalton 52.
Woman's Journal/Hugh Johnson 121; James Merrell 45T; Polly Wreford 49B.

Except: Robert Harding Picture Library/Michael Jenner 24; Elizabeth Whiting Associates 52–3;
William Morris Gallery, London 65.

CONTENTS

Introduction 6

Kitchens 18

Dining Rooms 34

Living Rooms 52

Garden Rooms 70

Bathrooms 84

Bedrooms 102

Techniques and Equipment 120

Index 128

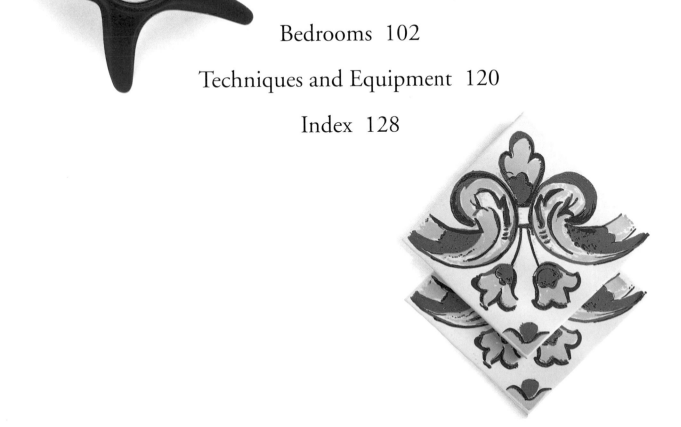

INTRODUCTION

ABOVE *Simple and inexpensive, covering storage boxes with wrapping paper can give surprisingly impressive results. Bright yellow labels make a vivid contrast with the blue.*

RIGHT *Traditional Christmas decorations look wonderful against blue and white. Here, blue gives this festive hallway a delightful naive charm.*

Decorating in Blue and White is the first in a series of colour coordinated books looking at the potential for using colour within the home. Combined with a variety of techniques, colour is used to accentuate and enhance decorations and home furnishings, bringing together traditional decorative styles with different crafts. *Decorating in Blue and White* will take you through the house giving inspiration and ideas for imaginative projects to fill each room.

Inspiration is provided by a colourful collection of photographs showing how different techniques have been used to enhance the home. Linked with this are easy-to-make projects for each room. The clear, step-by-step instructions will dispel any fears you may have about trying something new and will show you how to achieve these effects with the minimum of fuss and expense. The ultimate joy of this book is the fact that every design is accessible and affordable. Look out for bargains at sales, auctions or charity shops; rummage around in junk shops or at the back of your cupboards; invest in some dyes and paints and you'll have all you need to get started.

Over the last few years there has been a growing awareness of what can be achieved with simple paint and fabric techniques. And with the prohibitive cost of a professional facelift, more and more people want to add decorative, personal touches to make their homes unique. This type of modification appeals to both men and women because it is essentially creative. An afternoon with some paint and a stencil can lift the barest wall, turning it into something special and, at the same time, give you immense satisfaction. Imagine serving salad from a bowl you decorated yourself, or slipping into bed under a quilt you spent many happy hours putting together. It's fun! So turn the pages of this book and move from room to room. You'll find something to stir your creative juices and want to try at least one of the techniques explained in *Decorating in Blue and White*. In fact, working in blue and white couldn't be simpler. With a limited colour palette you are free to experiment and discover the potential of this age-old combination. After all, craftsmen the world over have been doing so for centuries.

Blue has always been a popular colour to use in the home. In combination with white it always looks fresh and clean so it's ideal for kitchens and bathrooms. Vary the tones and it fits as happily in a classical drawing room as it does in a peasant farmhouse: from porcelain and fine china to naive bowls and pots. Its long history has secured it a place in everybody's home, and it is impossible to find a time when blue or blue and white was not a prevalent colour combination for household items, ceramics and textiles.

LEFT *Ceramic pieces of different styles and origins make an attractive display, unified by their blue decoration.*

RIGHT *Geometric tiles look clean and fresh-looking.*

Blue is the colour

Early civilizations discovered colours through the efforts of trial and error, using different minerals and vegetation as pigments for dyestuff. As basic technologies evolved so did the presence of an ever growing variety of colours. Most common among the early ones were those derived from plant extracts which tended to produce muddy browns and yellows. Blue, however, could be achieved in fabrics using woad or indigo.

During medieval times the herb woad was the most common plant used to create a blue dye. Hailing from Eastern Europe and the Balkans it was used by dyers to produce single colour cloths. In France and Italy it was an important commodity: tight restrictions were placed on where and how it was grown and the finished fabrics were carefully inspected before they were sold. It set standards for the industry. Despite all efforts to maintain these and keep the woad trade buoyant it was not long before indigo, from India, appeared. Derived from a

delicate shrub of the legume or pea family, with oval leaflets and spikes of tiny reddish-yellow flowers, indigo had been used in Asia for centuries to colour cloth: early examples exist from 2500 BC. With the discovery of the passage to India, and the opening of trade routes, dyers were able to import indigo at low prices. Once it was readily available woad was rejected in favour of the strong colours achievable with the new plant, leaving many families destitute as their former livelihood disappeared. Word spread and indigo was introduced to Western Europe by the Dutch in the sixteenth century. For many years it was one of the staple industries of British India.

Working with indigo is fascinating. The strong-smelling dye looks muddy in the dye bath and the fabric emerges a dirty yellow colour. As it oxidizes in the air the colour changes through green to a rich blue.

Painting with pigments

Pigments used for paints and glazes were discovered from powders of minerals and ores. In the Neolithic period blue and green dyes were made using copper ore. The hues which could be produced ranged from green through to tones of blue-green. In the Middle East verdigris was produced by dissolving copper in vinegar to make a blue-green pigment. Lapis lazuli, a semi-precious gemstone, was used during the Copper and Bronze Ages. Crushed down to a powder it produced a rich blue pigment – ultramarine – but it was a rare mineral and hard to come by. (It was replaced by synthesized ultramarine in the early nineteenth century.) A blue produced from cobalt – a metal similar to iron – had been available in Persia for hundreds of years but it only became popular after it was introduced to China, where it was used as a pigment for painting on ceramics. Foreign trade was booming as were links with the West and there was a great demand overseas for Chinese wares. Ceramics decorated with ornate blue and white designs became sought after all over the world and cobalt became one of the most used pigments for people wanting to imitate this trend. It continued to be popular and with the advent of synthetic pigments in the eighteenth and nineteenth centuries, Prussian blue – an iron compound – and synthetic ultramarine were discovered, giving a greater choice of medium for working in blue and white.

LEFT *A plain chair can be made special by adding cushions. Here stripes create a dramatic effect.*

RIGHT *Dragging a rich deep blue on to these walls makes a marvellous foil for the gilt detail in the picture frame and candelabra.*

Around the world in blue and white

Once methods for making the dyes and pigments had been discovered and the trade routes between countries opened up it was an exciting time for anyone wanting to work with a single colour on white, be it on fabric, ceramics, wood or walls. The white became the canvas and the blue the drawing medium. It was a relatively inexpensive colour to work with as the raw materials were readily available and so was used in a variety of contexts, from peasant ware to stylish household items for the upper classes. The combination was particularly strong in ceramics from the fifteenth century onwards. Painting in colours began in China during the Tang Dynasty (AD 618–906) when pigments that could be fixed at high temperatures started to be used. The colours achieved by this method of firing were strong and uniform and the style was emulated by the Europeans once they, too, had mastered the technique. The pottery made was utilitarian, used in the kitchen and the storeroom. These medieval wares were not meant for ornament and consequently there are few examples remaining. By the fifteenth century, however, lead and salt glazing had been discovered and ceramic ware became a much more luxurious commodity. It received a fresh value during the seventeenth and eighteenth centuries when reputed artists started painting on china. Frederick van Frijtom of Delft in Holland was famous for his blue on white work.

Mediterranean pottery was commonly decorated in blue with bold strokes depicting stylized birds, plants and animals. In Spain and Italy these traditional designs were used as decoration for practical household jugs and pots. The style was also adopted by other European countries and the intrinsic motifs

were incorporated into many different designs. The sixteenth century potters from Faenza in Italy took the technique into France and Holland and then on to England. The style was known as *faience*. In Holland itself the work was concentrated in Delft and this is what we now know as delft ware. In Germany and Switzerland too blue and white pottery became desirable.

In England an English delft ware was being produced. Worked on earthenware, the designs were first painted white and then decorated with blue motifs, often with a mottled blue glaze. The objects made were drug jars, wine bottles, punch bowls and decorative display plates. The plates were usually commemorative, celebrating some of the great events of the time, and their heraldic motifs and formal designs meant they soon became collectors' pieces. With the Chinese influence, however, styles became more sophisticated and the decoration neater and more formalized.

Mid-eighteenth century potters in England started working in white on a bluish background: *bianco sopra bianco*, a technique thought to have come from Sweden. In Staffordshire 'scratch blue' was perfected where engraved flowers or birds were filled with powdered cobalt and subsequently fired. More refined designs of rococo figures and florals (characterized by their delicate, curved forms and slender proportions) followed – and so the developments continued. Wedgwood made his name with his jasperware in which white on blue was predominant and which is still popular today, and the Staffordshire and Worcester potteries excelled.

From the sixteenth century the technique of faience became popular in many countries of Europe. This is a superb display of English delftware.

The age of designers

There is a school of thought which says that the advent of transfer prints was a step backwards in the progression of a quality design. Transfer printing enabled the potteries to produce a series of wares with the same design; the artwork was produced only once. This development went hand in hand with the Industrial Revolution in Britain at the beginning of the nineteenth century as the money men looked for quick and easy ways to develop their businesses. The artist's role was jeopardized. The period after the Industrial Revolution was a telling time for design. Prior to this, craftsmen followed their trade but few were well known; styles were acclaimed but the artist rarely acknowledged. (It wasn't until the

Enjoy making your choice of printed fabrics to enliven an otherwise plain and low-key room.

twentieth century that a token number of these earlier craftsmen received recognition for their work.) However the Arts and Crafts movement, which was established in the nineteenth century, turned the position around and created a new genre of designers.

William Morris, a British designer, artist and poet, was the main instigator behind the Arts and Crafts movement. He strove for quality, form and function in his designs because he felt that mechanization had created a glut of inferior products, with no pride for craftsmanship. Many of his compatriots embraced this concept and began producing hand-crafted designs of quality. Morris is famous for his wallpaper and fabric prints and his unique designs can still be bought today. He was also a lover of blue. Two of his most used colours were grey-blue and green-blue. From the Arts and Crafts stable came William de Morgan, famous for fantastic ceramics and his use of a lustre glaze. He too favoured blue. Used with the glaze the colours were rich and vibrant, iridescent like mother of pearl. Simple, well-crafted styles with beautiful finishes were synonymous with the Arts and Crafts movement and brought a fresh impetus to the field of design. Previously, artists had always received the accolades. Now it was the turn of the designer.

Twentieth century style

The twentieth century has brought many new looks to our homes, with styles such as Art Nouveau, Art Deco and Cubism bringing ever more designers to the fore. The idea of interior decorating isn't new. From the fifteenth century onwards designers were employed to style homes. They would decide on colours, furniture, pictures and ornaments and a room would be turned into a show piece. It was, though, a luxury only afforded by the rich. Nowadays, with more disposable income and a far greater choice than ever before, everyone can give their home a certain style, but that style should be of their choosing and preferably their making.

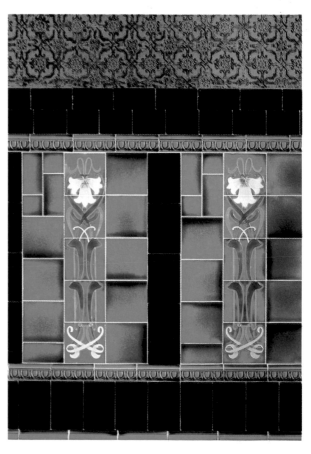

ABOVE *The clear shapes and strong colours of Cubist painting and Art Deco style are complemented by the blue frieze around the chimneybreast.*

RIGHT *Rich turquoise and cobalt are typical of turn-of-the-century Art Nouveau tiling.*

The years of the Second World War were lean and design was not given much consideration, but the period after the war brought with it a renewed interest in the home. The boom in the United States during the 1950s gave birth to a consumer society across the globe. The new medium of television brought images of an ideal home and a perfect family – everybody's dream. Advertisers were selling the dream and people wanted it – and it was not just in America, it was worldwide. In Britain, for example, the long years of rationing were over and people wanted material things. There was little concept of individual style: mass produced, low cost furniture and ornaments found their way into the homes of millions.

The designers of the time wanted to create something new and different, something that had never been done before. By providing stylish coordinated furniture and furnishings they were doing all the thinking. You didn't need an interior designer, all that was needed was the skill to mix and match. Wallpapers, soft furnishings, paints and furniture were all geared towards enabling you to create your own personal look and people loved it. After the psychedelic Sixties and the popularity of earth tones during the 1970s, the 1980s saw a revival of interest in colour – blues, greens, reds and pinks were everywhere. Designers were looking to the past for their inspiration and themes – from the rustic country feel of a Provence farmhouse to the luxurious opulence of the Middle East. There were no rules. Ideas for the home were diverse and extremely exciting. Home decorating was fashionable with shops and stores dictating colour and trends to the masses. Many followed the crowd but a few wanted something more – they didn't want to be dictated to. These were the people hunting through junk shops, painting on their walls and furniture, mixing old with new and kitsch with conventional. Others admired the unique looks they created and wanted to achieve the same but didn't know how – it was safer to buy ready-made. The stores realized there was an interest in hand-made crafts and started stocking traditional peasant crafts, hand-painted bowls, patchwork quilts; all manner of things to buy which looked home-made. Now, though, people are tempted to try and see if they can make these things – and more – themselves. With a revived interest in home crafts the media are meeting the demand by producing books, magazines and television programmes to show people how anyone can create the personal touch at home.

Blue today

As for blue, it's currently benefitting from a revival. The freshness of blue with white works well in every home. It's an easy combination to live with and the range of shades is immense. You can recreate a Victorian bathroom with a white bath, an antique blue and white jug and wash bowl, hand painted tiles and a doorplate. For the kitchen look for antique drug jars: they make wonderful storage for food. Bright blue glass pharmacy bottles are good for vinegars and oils. Display them on a shelf in plain view. Scour your local antique shops for a hand-painted ceramic slab and show it off. If you want a more modern look use potato prints to decorate plain white tiles. The repeats are easy and this technique takes no time at all. You don't need to be an artist, all you need is some imagination. In the lounge create a decorative effect by painting seashells and displaying them in a clear glass bowl. Stencil a frieze around the

When you have mastered the art of stencilling you can create beautiful decorative results with ease.

walls. You can buy ready-made stencils and once you've mastered the technique of stippling with a stencil brush, you'll create perfect effects time after time. If it goes wrong – that's character! If you're really not happy, paint over it and start again. Use tie dye to make a chair throw. Commercial dyes are easy to use: you can even buy them to use in the washing machine. By folding and pleating the fabric you can create subtle patterns. Stitching through the fabric and gathering it will give a different effect again. Look for inspiration from books on the crafts of Africa, where they have mastered the art of tie dyeing; and why not use indigo for a truly authentic look? It's messy and smells, but is well worth the effort as it looks wonderful. In the bedroom, why not make your own quilt? It's a large project but immensely satisfying. If you don't have the patience for that, cheat. Buy patchwork panels and sew them together or use fabric paints and

paint the design on to the fabric. Coordinate your furniture by first painting it and then stencilling each piece. Be brave on your walls: use the rich luxurious colours that paint companies make now. Play with them and see what you can achieve. Use a sponge to give your walls texture. Rag roll your cupboard doors. The techniques are so simple – all that is required is a little education, some time and lots of enthusiasm.

And, most importantly, remember to look around you. When you go to somebody else's home look how they've decorated: use magazines, use books, talk to people about your plans. Once your head is full of potential ideas you'll find that your inspiration flows. You'll probably find that, once you start looking and taking on board all the possible combinations, your ideas have changed. This is good; it means that your original concept is developing and that you are starting to think like a designer.

Look out for Victorian and Art Nouveau-style tiles at your local DIY store.

KITCHENS

ABOVE *Buying or making matching accessories can be a cheap and cheerful way of giving your kitchen a facelift.*

It is said that you can tell a lot about a person from their choice of kitchen. There are fundamental rules about creating one yet these basics only serve to lay the foundations; from there on in the kitchen becomes personal. It is rare that you'll find any two the same. Even with the availability of mass produced, fitted kitchens people manage to stamp their own with individuality. Whether it be by the choice of storage jars or where they decide to put their pots or knives, each one is unique. With this in mind, the kitchen opens many opportunities for creative decorating. Historically it has always been the centre of domestic life with idyllic images of fresh bread rising in the grate, a pot of hot stew bubbling on the stove and a big table surrounded by happy friendly faces. In reality, of course, this isn't always the case, but the kitchen carries with it still a legacy of being a friendly room that is open to all. Simple decorative techniques can add to this feel, making an ordinary room warm, comfortable and homely; in short, making something extremely special.

RIGHT *Today's version of the traditional country kitchen benefits greatly from simple touches of blue.*

18

Kitchens and colour

A kitchen is a workroom. No matter what you decide to do to it, at the end of the day its purpose is purely practical. It is also, however, a room in which you spend a lot of time so it's important that the atmosphere and work environment are comfortable and pleasant. A dark room may seem oppressive so when considering decoration you should consider light, the effects of colour with light and the aspect of the room itself. A north-facing room will always seem darker than a south-facing one, but you can lift the sombreness with clever

use of colour. If you've the luxury of a large room, your job is made easier. Many households nowadays have only a small kitchen, so a further consideration should be how to make the best use of the available space. With any kitchen you should have a working triangle: the cooker, fridge and sink should form a triangle with each other for ease of use and for safety. Outside of that, decorating decisions should be personal.

The advent of the fitted kitchen has made kitchen design simple. A designer's job becomes like putting together a jigsaw puzzle – working out the size of the room and then finding suitable units to fit. Many are turning back to the more traditional style of kitchen, only with the luxury of modern appliances to make the mix more practical. Even enamel sinks, once loathed and abhorred, are finding their way back into the modern kitchen, recreating a simplistic style held in high regard by the admirers of country life. This country style works well in a kitchen as the tones are warm and the feel friendly – exactly what is needed.

Blue and white have always been colours strongly associated with the kitchen. The bright, clear tones brighten up even the darkest rooms and the connection with clear blue skies and bright sunny days adds a lightening touch. Whitewashing used to be the norm for kitchens. As workrooms they were not show pieces and were given practical rather than decorative makeovers. The only touches of colour seen in older kitchens tended to be blue or the texture of a solid wood, with blue-tiled recesses being a particular favourite. This was common in kitchens the world over.

Collect pieces of old blue and white china and fill a kitchen dresser with it to make a dramatic impact.

LEFT *Light blue panelling gives this unusual modern kitchen a timeless feel.*

BELOW *Fitted units make good use of space, and cool blue with white handles creates a pleasant working environment for the cook.*

DISTRESSED CABINET

Create a Provençal feel for your kitchen cupboard by using the following techniques with rich cobalt blue.

1 First, use knot sealer: choose dark for dark woods and clear for blond woods. Paint the knots carefully to keep them as small as possible. Paint straight on to the bare wood a coat of blue emulsion made by mixing some vinyl matt emulsion extra deep base with standard acrylic white undercoat.

When it is completely dry take an ordinary cheap white household candle and rub this over the areas where you want the blue to show through, taking into consideration the areas of natural wear. Apply the wax generously (fig.1).

2 Now paint your chosen second colour – white knocked back with a little burnt umber. Then, when the paint is almost dry, take medium sandpaper and carefully rub in the direction of the grain (fig.2). Then do the same with wire wool.

3 To soften the complete effect mix burnt umber and raw sienna with white spirit and a dash of black paint and apply over the cabinet with a brush. To finish rub over with beeswax for a lovely lustrous glow.

In Moorish art, blue and white were used together with scrolls, motifs and decorative swirls on buildings, ornaments, textiles and mosaics – it was an instantly recognizable style. Traditional blue and white decoration can still be found all over Spain as a result of the country's invasion by the Moors many centuries ago. As well as being used on the façades of buildings, the combination found its way into the home. With the hot, arid Mediterranean climate you might expect parched, scorched earth colours. But blue and white with touches of red and vibrant yellow brought both a fresh coolness and colour to a worn environment. When Christopher Columbus discovered America in 1492, he took with him elements of this style which was by now widespread. Mexicans had been using blue for centuries,

The magnificent Leighton House in London was decorated like a moorish palace, a style that was highly fashionable in the late nineteenth century.

usually in combination with other vivid colours, and by using traditional Mexican motifs with the addition of the Moorish influence a new style was created. Angular geometric detail was used for pots, tiles and textiles. Blue and white tiles covered kitchens. They were colourful, practical, easy to clean and the ceramic against the walls kept rooms cool – essential for a kitchen which could become extremely hot when cooking. Tiling also added insulation and so worked both decoratively and functionally.

Blue became a colour of domesticity. Checked drapes hung from kitchen windows with coordinated cloths and a vase of brightly coloured flowers gracing the table. Simple yet stylish colour was used to create a homely atmosphere. This was a concept embraced by the colonial settlers who had uprooted and wandered into a vast new country, with no base, no home to speak of. They needed to create a home and a culture. Much effort was expended turning simple settlements into something which felt like home. All the accoutrements were added – many of them stitched. Tiny printed muslins and crisp cottons were used for samplers, quilts, curtains, cloths... personal touches which would enhance the environment, and many were in blue and white. The style was simple, often copying the familiar trends of European furniture with a more naive rendition. Furniture was often painted and a common colour for this was a deep grey-blue, known nowadays as colonial blue. The American settlers were establishing their roots and with it a legacy. Examples of their work survive to this day.

Matching checked curtains and tablecloth give a fresh, homely atmosphere in a kitchen-dining room.

Simple touches are easy to add to your own kitchen, turning an ordinary environment into something quite spectacular which needn't cost the earth. Gingham is inexpensive and it's a straightforward job to run up a pair of curtains. Café curtains, for instance, have a certain elegance and offer privacy in a more attractive way than net curtains: use brass rings and hang them from a matching pole. This classy look can be achieved in only a few hours. Alternatively, you can add a gathered pelmet.

DECORATED BOWLS

*Use a sponging technique and ceramic paint to create
a modern, simple design for kitchen bowls*

1 Take a sponge and using a pair of scissors cut it up into 1 inch squares. These will be used to print the design on to the bowls. You will need several squares because they quickly get clogged with paint. Make sure the bowls are clean and free from dirt before starting to print.

2 Now pour some ceramic paint into a flat dish. Dip your sponge into the paint, making sure that it is not overloaded with colour. If you find the sponge has too much colour on it, first dab it on to a cloth or piece of kitchen roll. Working from the top of the bowl towards the bottom, work your pattern over the upturned bowl. Leave an equal space between prints to create a chequered pattern. As you reach the bottom you'll find the spaces need to be smaller.

3 When you've finished the chequers let the paint dry. Finish the design by using a fine paint brush to draw a line around the rim edge of the bowl and a thicker brush to paint a wide band above the chequered pattern. Ceramic paint is ideal for decoration but it should not be used on articles which will be washed and used often.

This use of blue and white, with wide double doors, has made a feature out of a small space.

Emphasizing the idea of simple decoration being successful, you need look no further than some of the Mediterranean peasant styles which have become so popular in recent years. Rural environments were not led by fashions and trends, they were created from the heart, with the resources to hand. With the natural inspiration of sun, sea, sand, green fields and trees it's understandable that people should want their homes to imitate their surroundings, recreating something familiar with which they feel comfortable. Green was a difficult colour to dye but by using pigment people could recreate the rich blue of a Mediterranean sky – a refreshing tone which exudes an air of calm. In rural America, Spain, Portugal, Italy, Greece and France there was a profusion of blues on painted furniture, pottery and ceramics, panelling and elegantly crafted tiles.

ABOVE *A little line decoration turns a pair of ordinary jugs into something unique.*

LEFT *A cottage kitchen is brought to life with glorious cornflower blue woodwork.*

BELOW *Mediterranean style is always popular because of its simplicity and bold use of cobalt.*

29

POTATO PRINTED BLIND

*Create a unique effect on a traditional roller blind
with only a potato and some acrylic paint*

1 On a piece of paper make a rough sketch of how you want the finished blind to look. Now lay out the clean blind on a large firm surface such as a table, and hold the corners down with some DIY masking tape. Then take a ruler and pencil and, following your rough sketch, lightly mark the places where you want to put your potato prints. In this way you will end up with straight lines and an even distribution of prints.

The template for the spot pattern can be something as simple as a coin. If you want a spot of a different size, take a pair of compasses, draw a circle on a sheet of paper and cut it out with a pair of scissors.

To transfer the spot shape to your potato, first take a sharp kitchen knife and cut off one side of the potato cleanly and level. Now press your coin or paper circle to the cut side and use a craft knife or the same kitchen knife to scrape away the surrounding potato to a depth of about ½ inch.

Finally, remove the paper or coin template.

2 Put some acrylic paint in the bottom of a flat dish. Mix it with water until it has a firm yet fluid consistency. Use a spare piece of potato to test the consistency. When you are happy, dip your precut potato into the paint. Dab off any excess and print your first spot on to the fabric. Follow your plan and pencil guidelines to transfer the design on to the blind. When the paint is dry you can seal the design with a clear matt varnish.

The country communities had created a style of their own and none more so than in Provence, a sleepy rural idyll in southern France which to this day evokes tranquillity, with its warm climate and leisurely pace of life. It's an area rich in indigo, so it's not surprising that there were so many blues produced here. The simplicity of the Provençal style is one of its strongest points. Colour washed furniture left to crack and age – and not designed to make a fashion statement – has become universally popular. The look can be recreated by first painting your piece of furniture, then covering the areas you wish to show through with wax. Paint a second coat in a contrasting colour and using wire wool rub away the top coat from the areas you have waxed. This will bring the undercoat through. It works best if you use a dark colour for the undercoat, with a white or lighter colour on top. Blue and white make a terrific combination for this effect. It's a good technique for prematurely ageing furniture, although in Provence or any other rural environment the furniture would have aged naturally through time, use and exposure to the elements.

Also connected with Provence are vibrant blue printed cottons used both for clothing and in the home. The blues, strong and rich, used to be created using the abundant supply of indigo in the area – denim, too, hails from this part of France. The traditional peasant dress from Provence is instantly recognizable by the use of the blue dyed fabrics with small motifs in gold, red and brown regularly printed on the deep blue cloth. In combination with larger prints it is also used for curtains, cloths and soft furnishings. Wandering around the area you will still see exquisite examples of this type of work on display in people's homes. There is currently a fascination with traditional style and shops around the world are importing ethnic prints, so it is likely that, as well as seeing examples of this work in France, you will be able to find them in Great Britain, America, and many other countries too.

Ideas

In a kitchen you can use fabric in many ways. The obvious choice is for curtains – the Provence prints would work beautifully set against a white background – yet you could coordinate these with other items bringing through a strong blue theme. Use the prints to make tea towels, bread bowl liners, oven gloves or lace-edged covers for the top of your preserve pots. Decorate your shelf edgings, either with strips of the coloured fabric trimmed with a heavy lace, or by tracing off one of the patterns from the fabric and turning it into an embroidered shelf edging. Change the cupboards themselves by giving them a distressed finish. Pep them up with some colourful stencilling. And use bottles and jars filled with culinary delights to add to the picture. All these ideas are easy to master and could turn your kitchen into a Provençal palace.

Nothing looks more decorative in a large kitchen than a massed display of blue and white china. You can happily mix different blues, different patterns, antique and modern – the effect is always stunning.

DINING ROOMS

ABOVE *Why not paint a cutlery tray to match the rest of your dining room accessories?*

The early part of the twentieth century was a great period for the dining room. Food was in favour and the ultimate luxury for an evening's entertainment would be a dinner party. Course after course of lavishly prepared food would be brought to the table, served by waiters from silver salvers. It was a memorable social occasion enhanced by the company and the surroundings in which the food was served. Bone china dishes, cut glass, a crisp white cloth and candelabra all went to create an elegant social environment. Set apart from the drawing or sitting room, the dining room was probably the only room where family and friends came together, talked, ate and enjoyed each other's company, so its social significance was substantial. As this century has progressed, the dining room has lost some of its allure. Fast food and staggered working hours, with both partners out all day and eating at different times, have all added to the change. The dining room needs to be appealing, a room people will want to use throughout the day and in the evenings, a practical family room – not a showcase – to bring the life back to meal times.

RIGHT *Small decorative details can make all the difference between something ordinary and a room that's special in the festive season.*

Dining rooms and colour

Simple dining furniture in a white room can be enhanced by touches of blue.

Dining rooms are much under-rated and eminently under-used. It's a rare luxury these days to find houses with a room set aside purely for eating. All too often an extra room becomes a study or a workroom or a playroom for the children. Those without the extra room take a corner of the living room or kitchen and set it aside for eating. It's difficult then to decide whether the room should be decorated as a dining area, a living room or indeed as part of the kitchen. In many homes the dining table has a useful role as a space for setting up a sewing machine or a computer; rarely is it used for its original purpose. An open-plan lounge-diner is common, with the dining area an integral part of the lounge. As the furniture is pushed back to accommodate the television, the stereo and the family, the dining space becomes forgotten. Yet it can be exquisite when used for its proper purpose and it's important that this is not overlooked when replanning

space and deciding how it should be decorated. Make the space special. If you have a dining room, pamper it. So many of the historical wares worked in blue and white were designed for use in the dining room. These colours look fabulous against oak, mahogany and pine – one of the reasons the blue and white combination has always been so successful. Contemporary furniture screams for the uplifting impact of a touch of colour.

If you've a dining area, take the theme through from the room it's adjoining but change the tone, filter through the colours, to give one end a different feel from the other. While a warm blue may work in a living area you may want the colour in the dining area to be cooler. Lift the tone and graduate the sequence of colour. To keep the mood between the areas the same use a unifying border to link the room, a matching carpet throughout and, if you're using natural wood in the living area, carry it through to the dining room. A separate dining room has even greater potential. Make sure you have lots of cupboard space so that, if your dining room has to be multi-functional and you need to use it for entertaining, you can clear everything away and turn it from a workroom into the gastronomic haven for which it was intended.

RIGHT *If you are good at sewing why not re-cover your dining chairs for a new look?*

BELOW *Combining different shades of blue can lift the most restrained decor.*

HAND PRINTED TABLECLOTH

Potato printing can create some remarkable effects. By putting together simple elements a variety of finishes can be achieved

1 Use 100% cotton fabric because it takes dye well. To remove any finishing on the cotton wash the tablecloth, then iron it to make it flat and smooth.

Now draw out on sheets of paper how you would like the finished design to look . Use this as a guide to help you transfer the layout of the design to the cloth.

For the three individual elements of the design, trace off the small templates opposite on to a sheet of paper and then cut them out. Slice one edge off three potatoes with a kitchen knife (see fig.1 on page 30). Place one paper template on top of each flat edge, and cut away the surplus with a craft knife to a depth of ½ inch. For the dotted effect, gauge small, circular holes in the potato with a potato eye remover.

2 Put some fabric paint in a flat dish. Mix it with water until the consistency is firm but still fluid, testing with a spare piece of potato. Use a brush to cover the top of each precut shape with paint (fig.2). Transfer the design to the tablecloth, following your original design. When you have finished, fix the design by pressing the back of the cloth with a hot iron.

Trace these templates on to
paper. Cut around them
before fixing to the
potato.

Collectables on display

Bring the glamour back to meal times by using fine china and delicate glassware to add an air of luxury. The range and variety of fine wares available are phenomenal and you can use them for eating or – as in many a fine home – to display. Eighteenth and nineteenth century transfer printed ceramics are a collector's and decorator's dream. Displayed in cabinets, on dressers and walls, they take you back to a time when blue and white was at the peak of its

In the eighteenth and nineteenth centuries blue and white wares were made in Worcester, Liverpool, Bow and a number of Staffordshire factories.

popularity. English potters in Bow and Worcester took up the process by imitating Chinese motifs and subsequently created rural scenes with castles, landscapes and florals. Pure collectors look for perfect pieces, yet for the beauty of simply appreciating the blue and white wares you can collect disparate or slightly imperfect pieces which will not make too much of a dent in your wallet. A print was taken on transfer paper from an engraved copper plate

and this print was then transferred on to the ceramic. Fixed in an oven, the ceramic was then glazed. Cobalt was the only pigment which could be fired at the high temperatures needed for this technique so the wares were inevitably blue. Early examples had the transfer printed after glazing. These items were exported extensively after the Napoleonic wars. North America was a prime customer for blue and white printed wares and, from 1830, the industry took off in America. Unlike textiles of the period, many examples of this style have survived to become highly prized and collectable.

The Wedgwood Influence

With blue on white ceramics having been so popular during the eighteenth and nineteenth centuries, it was an exciting development when reputed potteries changed their focus and instead of working on a white background, started using the stronger colour as the base and white as detail. Neo-classicism – an aesthetic movement and artistic style which came to the fore in the latter part of the eighteenth century – embraced a renewed interest in Greek and Roman antiquity fuelled by the discoveries of classical remains in Pompeii and Herculaneum in Italy. Contrary to other classical revivals, the designers of the time were not trying to emulate traditional classical styles, but were looking forward and trying to create something new using classicism as a trigger and inspiration. It was one of the first periods in history where decorative and applied arts were influenced by fashion. From 1770 onwards ceramics too were influenced by this style, with Josiah Wedgwood at the fore of the movement. Wedgwood, a master potter from England, started his business in 1759, establishing his hold of the neo-classical designs and bringing a renewed vigour to the potteries of the time. He was an innovator, best known for his 'basalt', unglazed black stoneware; 'rosso antico', a hard red stoneware; and his 'jasperware', a fine white stoneware which could be coloured through the body and which he stained blue, green, mauve or yellow. The cameo-type relief worked in white on these wares was in typical neo-classical style; evidence that its simplicity and elegance are ageless shows in the fact that these wares are still being produced today and are in great demand. Antique Wedgwood is also highly sought after and yet, for a fraction of the cost, you can buy brand new! Wedgwood ceramics sit well in a dining room environment. Set on a crisp damask cloth the delicate colour of the bowls, pots and vases creates a striking display. Fine detail and exquisite decoration should secure this work pride of place in your home.

A blue and white dinner service looks beautiful against polished wood in a traditional dining room.

STENCILLED FRAME INSERT

Reverse a stencilling technique to create a decorative border for a picture mount.

1 Trace off the template shapes on page 44. Using a tacky spray mount spray the reverse side of your cut out shapes. Stick them on to your mount wherever you want the area to remain white.

2 Using a hard stencil brush dab your colour over the frame. Then use a second, lighter colour for contrast.

3 Peel off the shapes to reveal your finished frame insert. To finish, cut the insert from the frame with a craft knife, first measuring the size of hole you require. Use a set square (ideally a metal one) to ensure that you cut the corners at accurate right angles.

Templates overleaf

A touch of glass

Distinctive blue glass – limpid, rich and mesmeric like the colour of the deep Mediterranean – can still be found. Glass is coloured with the same pigments used for ceramics. Cobalt is used because it produces a strong colour and can withstand the high temperatures needed for the blowing process. By the beginning of the sixteenth century in Italy glass was being worked in blue, purple and green but it wasn't until the eighteenth century that it became truly popular. At Potsdam in North Germany deep blue and green glass was produced, although the glassworks was most famous for its ruby red which was highly valued. In Bristol in England, deep blue glass was made which was used for practical purposes – mainly bottles and vases – and these are still widely sought after. In a modern home the rich colours liven up a room either displayed as single items, where the shape and smooth texture stand alone, adding classy detail to a room or en masse, when the profusion of stimulating tones is irresistible. In America, during the eighteenth century, apothecary blue evolved. It was a pale greenish-blue used for medicine jars and was especially popular in the South. If you can find an example of this individual glass it would create a spectacular centre piece, filled with coloured glass beads or used as a vase, brimming with vivid flowers.

ABOVE *Glass coloured with cobalt makes a distinctive ornament that still blends well with other decorative pieces in a display.*

RIGHT *Mix blue with gold, using glass paints, to add a touch of drama when you entertain.*

CURTAIN TIEBACKS

*Use Indonesian ikat effect silk painting for
curtain tiebacks*

1 Enlarge the template opposite to make your own personal crescent-shaped template: it should be long enough to wrap loosely round one of your curtains when drawn back. Pin your template to a piece of dupion silk and draw carefully round it with a soft pencil so that you have two shapes to work on, making sure that the right side of the fabric is always uppermost.

2 Make sure the silk pieces are held firmly down on a flat surface. Using diluted fabric paints, apply your design. Chevron shapes worked across the grain of the silk, with gaps between colours, will give an ikat effect. Use water to encourage the paints to bleed and resemble the piece-dyed yarns used in traditional ikat work. Add detail with gold fabric paint.

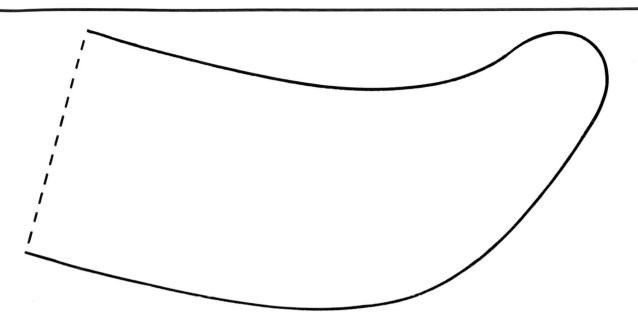

3 When you've finished painting cut out the tiebacks from the rest of the silk. Cut two pieces of interlining, and two pieces of plain silk or other backing fabric, the same size as the decorated pieces. For each tieback baste the three elements together and bind round the edges with a satin ribbon. Fix a curtain ring to each of the four ends, and attach to a hook in the wall or window frame in the usual way.

Ideas

Pottery, glass and ceramics are always at home in a dining room whether it be practically or for display – it's a room which lends itself to collectables. You could create your own heirloom pieces and you don't have to be an artist to achieve some spectacular results. On ceramics use stencils to repeat a pattern on a dinner service. Cut a design into a sponge, load it with dye and create your design this way.

Alternatively, cut shapes and pictures from pieces of paper and arrange them decoratively on a plate. Then, using a paint brush, splatter the exposed area of the plate with two or three different tones or colours. Lift the paper carefully. You will achieve a reversed stencilling effect. Be bold, use colour dramatically; use a paint brush to create stylized or geometric

Naive decorative effects are easy to achieve with sponges, stencils and ceramic paints.

images. If you want a more structured look but don't feel you can draw, trace the image you'd like to see and transfer it on to your plate, then simply paint in the detail. Line up all the plates you have created and display them against a natural wood dresser. Look around your local markets and second hand shops for examples of antique blue and white work and display it with the new designs you've created yourself.

Look for the old apothecary jars and medicine bottles. They are universally available. You could even go into an old pharmacy and ask if they have any hidden away under the counter – it's surprising what can be found lurking in a store cupboard. Keep an eye open for interestingly shaped glass bottles: filled with coloured oils and used as candles they can be picturesque. If you'd like to decorate your own glass, invest in some glass paints. Modern craft glass paints are easy to use and with them you can create subtle yet vibrant results. Find an image you'd like to reproduce and place it behind the glass, using a resist paint around your outlines. Then simply fill the other areas with colour to create glass with an iridescent, Tiffany feel. You could cut scraps and stick them inside a glass bowl to face outwards, giving the effect of a reversed découpage. The possibilities with glass are endless yet the medium is so elegant it could be considered vulgar to change the balance and form. Why not simply display your cut crystal and allow the light to refract through prisms of rainbow colours?

ABOVE *With a little sewing technique you can transform the appearance of an upright dining chair. This is particularly useful if your dining area is part of your sitting room.*

RIGHT *Blue and white checks and stripes always look fresh and appealing on tablecloths and napkins.*

DECOUPAGE BOX LIDS

*Use scraps and varnish to produce an elegant
Victorian effect box*

1 Buy a set of Shaker-type
boxes from your local craft
shop. These boxes are currently
very popular and extremely
useful. Paint over each of them
with a coat of indigo acrylic
paint. This opaque paint will
cover them well. If you find it
necessary give them a second
coat. Each one will take about an
hour to dry.

2 Cut some motifs from
wallpaper borders, and
arrange them attractively on the
box tops. Run a pair of scissors
across the wrong side of the
motifs. This will make them curl
towards the back and ensure
they stick firmly on to the
surface. Using a PVA glue stick
your cut out shapes in place.

3 Let the glue dry before finishing. To finish you can coat the boxes with either the same PVA glue, which will dry clear, or two coats of light pine varnish. Leave for at least 24 hours to dry.

LIVING ROOMS

ABOVE *Teamed with gold and white, rich royal blue creates an elegant and luxurious look. Deep maroon makes an exciting contrast.*

RIGHT *Matching upholstery and curtains help to create visual unity in a room.*

There's never been a room quite so versatile as the living room. Until the twentieth century it never really existed. Houses had drawing rooms and games rooms, dining rooms, libraries and music rooms, but never a room which brought together all the social niceties – a room for relaxing, a room for living in. In smaller homes the kitchen tended to be the focus with a chair or chairs in front of the fire. With the technological and leisure advances throughout the twentieth century – the television, radio, stereo and video – there is now a need for a room in which to wind down and enjoy the luxuries of modern life. The rarest luxury of all must be the time available to do just this. The leisure society has brought with it a new, self-indulgent need for comfort so ultimately the living room has to be extremely welcoming. It's the room into which most visitors will be invited, a room from which others will identify your tastes and preferences, therefore – unless you're feeling reserved and inhospitable – it should be warm, all-embracing and friendly

Living rooms and colour

Of all the colours and tones you could use within a room, the living room offers the most scope for using these. In order to create warmth you might expect to have to use tones of red, orange and yellow, using blues and greens only for a cooler environment. Although these are the fundamental rules governing colour, by thinking about and using tone and hue, the shape of a room, the way it's facing and the secondary colours you use to enhance and lift it, you can achieve an abundance of striking effects, making cool colours warm and warm ones cool. In a living room blues tend to work better in combination with other colours. The colour itself is cool, yet when you consider its air of refreshing calm it's ideal in a room for relaxing. Rich ultramarine walls, with white woodwork, a wood panelled floor and pale blue upholstery would create a peaceful, welcoming environment. Coupled with hand-stitched cushions and drapes, the total combination would be strong yet classically stylish. Use a flat white to raise the ceiling and make the room feel more airy. For a lighter touch use tones of pale blue and azure in combination with white and a dark wood – blues always work well against wood. It's a traditional combination in Scandinavian countries where you'll find blues complementing wood in many homes.

Consider, too, what you require from your lounge. Is it to be an aesthetic space? Will it be somewhere people look but don't touch? Will you entertain? Have you got children? What are their needs? Do you need wall space for pictures? What electrical equipment have you got to accommodate? Do you want a unified, neat look, with niches and alcoves to hide the clutter – a place for everything and everything

in its place – or would you prefer something more lavish with drapes and throws, pictures and ornaments? The possibilities for stamping your own style on a living room are endless. It's not so private as a bedroom so you should choose an image you are happy to share; one that makes you feel confident and happy; one you can live with. Mantelpieces, table tops, shelves and cabinets are all places where you can display your favourite ornaments. Use plants to lift the environment and colour and lighting to create mood. With a living room used for so many different pastimes it's important that the furnishings fit their purpose. A comfortable sofa or chair in which to relax and a good light to work or read by are essential elements for the perfect living room.

LEFT *Cornflower blue woodwork accentuates the details of the checked throw on the sofa.*

BELOW *Using blue as a basis, you can mix different types of fabric prints successfully.*

NEEDLEPOINT CUSHION

*Make a beautiful needlepoint cushion with a
traditional Willow Pattern design*

1 Work the needlepoint
design on canvas using the
chart provided. It is worked in
three colours in tent stitch, with
backstitch outline in black. When
you've finished stitching cut out
the design, leaving an allowance
of ½ inch all around it.

2 To make up the cushion
you will need to cut a
gusset and a backing piece out of
a suitable fabric such as blue
velvet. The gusset should be
4 inches wide with ½ inch either
side for seams. The length
should equal the cushion's
circumference plus 1 inch.
Stitch the two short edges of the
gusset, right sides together, to
form a circle.

3 Working from the back of the needlepoint and gusset sew them to each other, right sides together. Cut the backing piece the same size as the needlepoint and sew it to the raw edge of the gusset, again right sides together. Leave an opening just large enough for you to turn the whole cushion right sides out. After filling with a circular cushion pad slip stitch the opening very neatly.

Chart overleaf

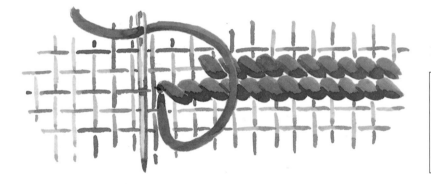

Follow this method to work your tent stitch.

When planning a room it is often difficult to imagine how it will look when completed. You may have an idea which in your head looks wonderful, but blithely set out with a roller and some wallpaper and you may end up with a room which looks nothing like your original concept. You can overcome this problem by creating mood boards before you start. Designers love mood boards, which help them to visualize the finished effect. Look through books and magazines and start collecting a folder of room sets. Collect samples of wallpapers, fabric and carpet swatches. Filter through them and pick out the ones which most closely resemble the effect you'd like to achieve. Mount your magazine cuttings with your paint samples and swatches on a board. Stand back and see how they start to form an overall picture of how your room may look. Mix and match your samples until you're happy with the effect. You are now ready to begin the transformation.

Once you've decided upon the tone for your room and how you plan to handle the decoration, you are free to fill it with pictures, ornaments and the like. With so many gift, antique and home shops about, you'll be sure to find something that will fit perfectly into your room. If, however, you're feeling creative, use the shops for inspiration and magazines for ideas so you can create something decorative yourself.

ABOVE *Details are important: use scraps of fabric to make patchwork chair cushions and matching ties.*

RIGHT *Dramatic tassels can be easily made to match and lift your decorations elsewhere in the room.*

The familiar and delightful Willow Pattern has been manufactured by many potteries from the eighteenth century onwards.

The Willow Pattern

There are innumerable possibilities for things you can make yourself, with inspiration coming from styles created over many centuries. A trip to the local library may unearth a design which has always fascinated you. One of the most popular blue and white designs which has been emulated, copied and reworked is the timeless Willow Pattern. It has always been a favourite and even today its elegant styling complements many rooms. You'll find it worked on china, tiles, in needlepoint and it has even been used as the basis for wallpaper designs. The traditional design shows a pagoda standing by the edge of some water, with two flying birds and a boat. There's a fence at the front, behind which is a bridge on which there are three Chinese figures. The prominent willow tree overhangs the bridge. The pattern did not, in fact, come from China but is an eighteenth century English design. This example of chinoiserie became more standardized in 1830 and a story was even invented by the British potteries to explain what was going on in the pattern.

A wealthy mandarin had a beloved daughter, Li-Chi, for whom he wanted only the best. When he discovered that she had fallen in love with the man who used to be his secretary he was enraged and forbade their betrothal. The couple eloped but the mandarin went after them with a whip. He would have beaten them to death had not the guards intervened and turned the lovers into the pair of turtle doves which can be seen in the foreground of the picture.

Fabrics, prints and pattern

Just as the blue and white theme had become so popular in ceramics, during the seventeenth century it became popular for fabric printing. Ornate printed cotton and chintzes were much sought after and, when the trade routes opened up between countries at the turn of the sixteenth century, cottons and calicos were being brought back from the Far East and India. During the latter part of the seventeenth century pintados (Portuguese and Spanish cloths) and chintzes became all the rage among the aristocracy. The original fabrics were soon imitated and European mills started to produce cheaper and more widely available fabrics. One of the first factories was set up in Amsterdam in 1671. Cotton printing threatened other textile industries and the owners of these used their powers to impose bans on the printing and importation of the cheaper fabrics. Bans were in force in both England and France by the end of the seventeenth century but somehow Marseilles, in southern France, managed to avoid the ban and workshops were set up producing a range of block printed fabrics for the export trade. Calico printing became widespread after 1685 when the persecuted Huguenots fled France. There were many calico printers among them who took the tricks of their trade to other countries and factories were established in Berlin and Geneva.

Once the bans were lifted Toiles de Jouy began to be printed at Jouy, between Paris and Versailles. The distinctive style was created by using engraved plates to print in a single colour on to cotton fabrics. The prints were used widely throughout France for furnishing fabrics during the mid-eighteenth to nineteenth centuries, a fashion which was supported favourably by both Louis XVI and Napoleon I. Popular print colours were blue, red and violet. In countries not affected by the bans textile production expanded during the eighteenth century. The fast-dyeing technique using mordants (a form of colour fixer) caught on throughout Europe where the Oriental influence was still a strong inspiration.

British textiles profited by new ideas in the late eighteenth century when a 6ft x 2ft copper engraving plate was developed that enabled printers to create large dramatic and detailed pastoral scenes quickly. Then, with the advent of cylinder printing, production processes could be stepped up. Printed fabrics were widely used for furnishings and were being produced at alarming rates. Mass production was an inevitable result of the Industrial Revolution. Quality suffered and designs became less inspired with prints being churned out repeatedly.

A twentieth-century version of eighteenth-century elegance, enhanced by the use of blue which was as popular then as it is now.

VERDIGRIS CANDLESTICK

Recreate this age-old copper finish in three simple steps and fill your home with original antique effects

1 Using a mid-brown matt emulsion cover your candlestick with a base coat. Leave for an hour to dry.

2 To create the verdigris finish use two blue-green paints, the first light and the second darker. Using the first colour, stipple it over the base coat with a stippling or large stencil brush. Let it dry and repeat with the second colour.

3 Once the paint has dried you can use a stick of gold paint to highlight the features and detail. Rub on the gold paint with your finger.

Patterns on paper

Early drawliners from the Tudor period show signs of how printers used wood blocks and inks to create patterns on paper. It is possible that they may have been used to paper walls, but it would have been a time-consuming job as the sheets were no more than twelve inches square. It is more likely that wallpapers were developed in the seventeenth century. It was then considered fine to use paper to cover walls as an alternative to traditional textile hangings. The industry developed in England and by the middle of the eighteenth century vast quantities of wallpaper were being exported, especially to America, with the majority of designs taken from those seen on fabrics and printed on to the paper using the same techniques. Wallpaper design, however, was never truly mastered until the middle of the nineteenth century when William Morris took the quality of the design to task and significant improvements in textile and wallpaper production were made. Disillusioned

A comfortable armchair covered in a traditional print in a quintessentially English drawing room.

by the quality of workmanship he had seen at the Great Exhibition in London in 1851, Morris set about challenging design concepts. His ideas were not purely aesthetic; the work of his Arts and Crafts movement had social implications too. Having seen the effects mass production had on design and the fact that the craftsman was no longer really creating the craft for which he had been trained, Morris and his colleagues started to address this. They wanted the work of the craftsman to be the best that could possibly be achieved, bringing back all the skill which was so sadly lacking through the advent of machine production.

Morris himself, who was specializing in prints for fabric and wallpapers, reintroduced the block printing technique which had been overtaken by cylinder printing. Although cylinder printing was a quicker printing technique, registration was sometimes off, the colours occasionally muddied and there was no pride in the workmanship. By working with block prints Morris could meticulously check the registration to produce perfect repeats. The work of his company, Morris, Marshall, Faulkner and Co., had a dramatic impact on the public at the time and the name of William Morris became synonymous with good design. His original textile designs were influenced by medieval and Gothic art with strong pattern and regular repeats, drawing on nature. The mid-twentieth century saw a resurgence of interest in Morris's work, and his distinctive and timeless designs can now be found everywhere.

Morris's Apple wallpaper, designed in 1877, is typical of the graceful, curving plant forms that he favoured, in stark contrast to the hard, flat effects of contemporary mass-produced wallpapers and textiles.

RESIST CURTAINS

*Colour and texture are important in the home: these
hand-printed curtains will make a handsome feature
in your lounge or drawing room*

1 Use a coloured cotton fabric, and cut it to length so you have two drops. Lay out the curtains on a firm flat surface and use a large brush to cover both with a layer of thick flour and water paste. Making sure the fabric remains taut, leave it to dry. As the paste dries it will begin to crack and break, leaving tiny rivulets into which the dye will seep.

2 Using a fabric dye, paint over the flour and water paste. The paste will create a resist – where it covers the fabric no dye will seep through. Where the fabric peeks through, the dye will absorb and create a pattern on the base cloth. Leave the dye to dry.

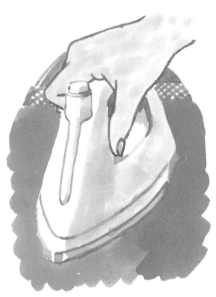

3 To fix the design, iron over the material from the back. Some fixing instructions may vary depending on the product you use. Read your dye packaging for specific instructions. Wash off the flour and water paste, preferably with a jet spray, and then wash and dry your finished fabric. You can now make it into any type of curtain you wish.

Decorative paint techniques

Pattern need not be fussy and overbearing. With the use of a few decorative techniques you can use pattern to achieve dramatic results without resorting to flamboyant use of excess colour – decorative paint effects can be simple. The living room is often a good place to use these techniques should you decide against using a flat paint technique or wallpaper. Sponging a wall gives a mottled effect. If you use a complementary colour to the base coat you'll achieve a two-tone effect. Working with a natural sponge gives the best result as the pores and shape are irregular. Build up the pattern by dabbing the sponge against the surface to be covered, applying the paint randomly over the complete area. Wait for your first coat to dry before working on a second. You could use this technique with two or three different tones or colours to create a marbled effect. In reverse, ragging produces a similar finish but instead of adding colour you take it away. Cover the area you want painted, then, using a loosely bunched rag, roll it across the surface to lift the excess paint. Use angular runs to avoid any hard lines. If the finish appears uneven, blot the heavier areas, which will lift more of the colour. Dragging, too, is popular for walls. First apply your paint or glaze and using a dragging brush pull back the paint, thus drawing off any excess. Use a long clean vertical stoke and try not to interrupt the flow. By using a thick gauge comb you can achieve a basket weave effect on your walls by first painting an area and then using the comb to work alternate vertical and horizontal lines. Combing is a technique that needs a little imagination and some initial practice. First work out how you would like the combing to look before applying it to the wall. It is controllable so, once you've decided upon the desired look, you can be confident that is what you'll achieve. There are also a variety of rollers available. Different cuts in the foam will produce some exciting paint effects from symmetrical even lines to ragging. For this you don't have to be artistic – just determined.

Pastel colours against white give a very modern look, with plaster shells adding detail.

Ideas

So now you've got prints for your furniture, techniques for your walls and curtains and a strong idea of how you'd like your living room to be. The themes are strong and the ideas flowing; all that's missing are the finishing touches. Look for inspiration to the work of the Arts and Crafts movement: their ethos is as relevant today as it ever was and some of the decorative work produced at the time was truly beautiful. A William de Morgan-type lustre-glazed bowl would make an attractive centre piece or a distinctive highly glazed Ruskin pot would stand tall on a mantelpiece. With peacock colours and exquisite detail this style of decorative art has created a legacy. Simply look to the past for inspiration for your decorations of the future. Appreciate the elegance of the work and in turn use the discovery to introduce style and proportion into your own environment.

Edwardian armchairs and a Victorian ironstone plate combine well with simple modern pieces.

GARDEN ROOMS

ABOVE *A profusion of colour will brighten any room, no matter what its aspect.*

RIGHT *Light pine is ideal in a conservatory, and the crisp geometric blue details in cushions, rug and chair covers work well with it.*

The ultimate room which brings together both indoors and out is a glass room from which you can enjoy the outside world. Looking out on to an area full of colour, taking in the rich blue of the sky, the strong greens of a pampered lawn and the jewel hues of flowers in full bloom is thoroughly rewarding. Long glass panes break down the barriers between the warmth and comfort of your home and the natural beauty of a summer's day. The two blend to bring inside an exceptional radiance of nature at its best. A room such as this can be a rich and colourful haven; from your choice of furniture to your use of decoration and ornament it's a room which crosses the divide between domestic and flamboyant. You've no need to temper your taste to fit in with the rest of the decoration because this room can stand alone. It's a fancy – a place to luxuriate. With the sun filtering through the panels, the genial conditions are perfect for winding down and simply appreciating the beauty around you.

Garden rooms and colour

More often than not a garden room or conservatory will lead through from a living or dining room. The atmosphere changes simply by walking through a door or down a step, for, even if the room is decorated in style with the rest of your house, as soon as you enter it you feel as though you're encroaching on the great outdoors. A light airy room offers great potential for those with a penchant for design. Using the view as a backdrop you can mix and match colours and textures which might not normally be appropriate in your other rooms. It may be an addition or extension to your basic house with the style chosen to fit with existing buildings or it may already exist, with deep French windows opening out on to an ample lawn. It offers substantial opportunities for using blue as a predominant theme. With the sky as a prime inspiration – its hue reflecting off the glass – you can use the colour quite confidently to enhance and create a cool, refreshing mood. Use cornflower for woodwork and deep cerulean blue tiles for floors, walls and recesses and recreate the breezy colours of spring.

Glass itself can be decoratively enhanced to bring colour into the room. If you have an existing room you may already have Art Deco stained glass. The technique was very popular throughout the late 1920s and 1930s, with a ray of sun design being a particular favourite for the glass in conservatories because of its obvious association with the outdoors. Stems of stylized flowers were also popular, as were geometric repeats.

Glass nowadays tends to be plain and could be enlivened with a little colour. If you'd like to reproduce the effect of stained glass it's very easy to do. A border of colour around the conservatory would add interest and lift the flatness of the glass. Find an image you like using reference books and magazines to help – adapting and changing it if necessary. Then stick your design on one side of the glass and trace the design on the other using a glass resist. If you're repeating the image, move it along the pane to work the next motif. Once you've drawn in all the outlines allow the resist to dry. You can then use glass paint to colour in the detail and the colours will remain inside the outline.

As the gateway between inside and out you'll need to pay particular attention to the flooring in this room. It should be durable and easy to clean as you'll find people wandering through without much consideration for your floor. Wood block, parquet, quarry tiles and stained floorboards all make attractive and durable surfaces. Couple this with an elegant rug decorated with a Moorish theme in hyacinth blue against white for a distinctive and original combination.

Easy chairs, coffee tables, lamps and an abundance of plants are all at home in a conservatory. Create an in-house jungle with climbers and foliage and display your prize blooms in all manner of decorative pots. Use naive hand-painted pots brought back from Mediterranean holidays, or an old enamel sink livened up with découpage, and look out for the eighteenth century-type blue and white printed chamber pots – they make fabulous plant holders. Bowls, dishes, vases and tureens filled with flowers all look exceptionally good in a room such as this. Glaze a terracotta pot with crackelogue varnish – available from decorative art suppliers – to create a sun-kissed, authentic Mediterranean feel. Use crisp whites, blues and yellows and mix them with rich green to exploit all the cheerfulness of a summer's day and keep the room light and bright to retain a certain freshness. White-washed walls and wood-stained floors conjure up the simplicity of an isolated beach house and will give your room an air of peaceful calm.

Cool shades of cobalt and azure lend a sense of freshness to this relaxing conservatory.

PAINTED FLOWER POTS

*An easy way to create an authentic Mediterranean feel
on plant pots*

1 Roll out some new clay with a rolling pin. Using a bucket, wrap the clay around the outside for your pot shape. Remove the bucket.

2 Before the pot is dry make an air hole in the base using a pencil. Leave your pot to dry properly.

3 Using acrylics, paint the pot blue, then add the white spots. Trace the template opposite and cut out the detail with a craft knife. Fix the template to the pot and draw around the box and figure. Move the stencil to draw the next motif, using the white paint to colour up the design. Finish by coating the whole pot with PVA glue for waterproofing.

Trace off this template on to acetate, which can then be cut into a stencil. Use it around the top of your pot. Adjust the spaces between the motifs so that they are evenly distributed around the size of pot you have selected.

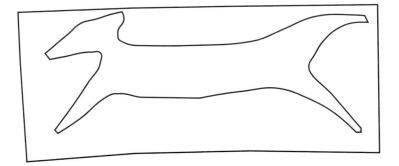

Capturing the Mediterranean

Pots work beautifully in a garden room and there are so many sources of inspiration from which to draw. For centuries the basic pot has been developed and improved upon by everyone from the indigenous communities in Africa and South America to the more technologically aware western societies. Pots were originally used to store foods and liquids to meet the demands of general living conditions in rural communities. Early vessels were made of wood and stone, with the use of clay coming slightly later. Clay was ideal because it was malleable and able to be worked

BELOW *Using easy paint techniques a cane chair, possibly a junk shop find, can be turned into a feature.*

into aesthetically pleasing shapes. People's innate desire to embellish everything led to simple decoration being used for pots and bowls. They discovered that they could make textural lines, grooves and incisions in the wet clay which, when it was dried and fired, would remain. A 'slip' finish was a popular peasant tradition, using dilute liquid clay to form a glazed effect on the pot. These slips could be coloured and trailed through a nozzle, drawn into, or drawn away with a sharp tool to uncover the base, or worked with a resist, such as wax, to bring out both the base and the colour. It was a versatile decorative technique which is still used in traditional peasant wares today. Glazes too were used and these could be coloured. A glaze has effectively the same make-up as glass and when compounded with metal oxides will produce a variety of colours. Blue has always been produced successfully because its pigments can withstand the high temperatures needed for firing, and the colour remains true. Metals – in oxide form – give colour to glazes: copper will give turquoise in a high soda glaze, iron gives a range of colours including a grey-green celadon blue and cobalt gives an intense but stable blue.

Create a Mediterranean look in a garden room or conservatory by mixing a range of colours to add drama and interest.

CHAIR CUSHIONS

Blue and white lino prints for patio furniture

1 Trace the design from this page and transfer on to the lino. Using a lino cutter, cut your design into the lino by chopping out the darker areas illusrated.

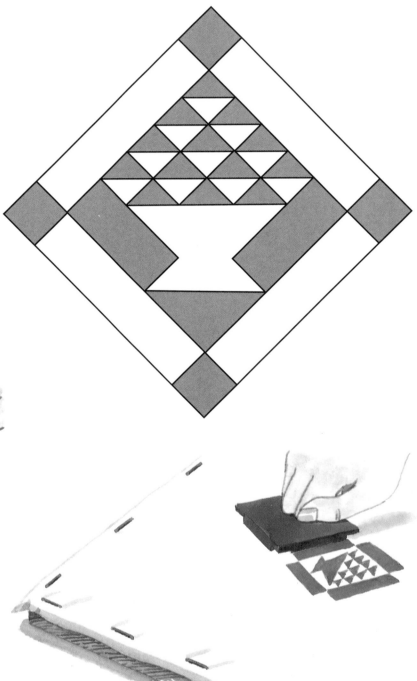

2 Using a roller, load the lino with fabric paint.

3 Print on to taut fabric. Heat fix the dye by ironing on the reverse.

Blue is a colour which has always been associated with peasant wares. The people were influenced by the Middle Eastern pottery which they came across as they travelled and they also had easy access to pigments. Many of the traditional Mediterranean wares were worked in blue on white. In Greece, potters used cobalt to produce designs which were sparsely decorated with circles and spirals filled with dark paint. One of the designs attributed to the Greeks is the characteristic key meander, which would run around the body of the pot. The style originated in Athens but soon spread throughout the rest of the country.

Many of the prevalent styles dominating the Middle East and Europe originated in the Islamic world, which was responsible for more refined decoration and enamelling. Islamic style strove for a lighter body and a whiter glaze which worked to a degree. These potters were never able to emulate the quality of Chinese wares as the clays available were inferior to those in China, so

Lush plant growth aims for the sky in this beautiful large conservatory and gives it an air of tropical luxuriance, while the elegant yet comfortable furnishings make it simultaneously the perfect sitting room.

ornament overtook the quality of the product itself. Syrian earthenware from the eleventh century used a white all-over slip decorated with an underglaze of cobalt blue, manganese and iron brown, black and copper green. The technique quickly spread to Egypt and Persia, and Persia soon became the centre for producing painted lustreware in a clear deep blue. From 1200 onwards Persian and North African potters were producing blue tiles for mosques and palaces, and examples of these distinctive tiles can still be found throughout the Middle East and, via Moorish and Spanish influence, South America. The styles are traditional and remain throughout the Middle East today. Trade routes and conquest have ensured that these types of wares are predominant in Europe, too.

Ideas

In the street markets of many Mediterranean towns and villages you can still find these traditional pots and bowls. They are as much a part of the countries' culture as the palaces and churches you see. Bring the pots back with you

and you can introduce a little ethnic style into your own home. The strong blues and simple designs make a dramatic impact and a collection of these decorative wares would lift a corner or ledge, bringing a truly Mediterranean air to your room. Fill them with flowers, beads or shells and make them a feature. Use simple yet classic furniture such as a table where you can snack or stop for a drink and give it some character by colouring the wood with a blue-tinged stain. This will give the effect of a glaze but allow the original wood to show through, so the result is very subtle. Stain the chairs to match and add elegant cushions with geometric patterns. Create the pattern either through your choice of fabric or by decorating it yourself. You could use stencils or a block print – a block is easy to repeat and the effect is most professional. The conservatory is a cool, relaxed room; remember this when you begin to consider how you'd like it decorated.

CLOUDED COFFEE TABLE

For a magical effect try this marbling technique and discover how deliciously easy it can be to create spectacular pieces of furniture

1 First seal all the knots with a knot sealer. Next coat with two undercoats, one of grey cloudy blue emulsion and a second coat of dark grey-blue oil-based paint (fig.1). When fully dry, sand it down carefully and wipe the residue off with a clean rag, wetted with clean white spirit. When this is dry, paint a fine film of boiled linseed oil all over and wipe off the surplus with a clean dry rag.

2 Make up a thinning mixture consisting of 1 part boiled linseed oil to 10 parts white spirit. Then make up a grey-blue from artist's oils in indigo, white, Prussian blue, cerulean blue and a little lamp black, added to oil-based white undercoat from a tin. Thin the oil colour until creamy, then, using a domed brush, paint large and small blobs all over the surface. Now take some white oil-based paint with a little of the grey-blue and mix until creamy with the thinning mixture. Working a section at a time, cover the whole table.

3 Dab a natural sponge dampened with white spirit over the surface. Make sure the previous colour has not dried before adding the next. Now mix a pure blue softened with a little black and white and flick evenly over the table with a paint brush to create an attractive splattered effect.

BATHROOMS

During the sixteenth century Queen Elizabeth I was said to be the cleanest woman in England. She proudly boasted that she took four baths a year so it's fair to assume that baths were not particularly popular at the time. Considering that cleanliness is considered 'next to Godliness' we've not always been that clean. Our ancestors devised many ruses to overcome having to wash, including using powder and scent to hide the dirt and the smell. From the promising beginnings of Roman baths, with heated water and plumbing, we definitely regressed. For many centuries bathing consisted of filling a tub from jugs, with water heated in pots – with no plumbing or heating this was the norm. It has taken nearly two thousand years for the bathroom to become as important a room as any other in the home. Nowadays we can luxuriate in the knowledge that if we turn on a tap, chances are there'll be hot water. We can fill the bath and watch the steam diffuse into the atmosphere, then, having made no effort at all, relax in the warm water, easing out all the stresses of the day.

RIGHT *Roll-top cast iron baths, whether antique or reproduction, are once again highly fashionable.*

Bathrooms and colour

Blue and white have always been colours associated with the bathroom. Our forebears extolled the virtues of this versatile combination and the earliest examples of bathrooms were covered, top to bottom, with blue and white tiles. The early nineteenth century saw some of the first houses built with rooms specifically put aside for bathing. These used transfer printed tiles for decoration and the ceramic fixtures produced were decorated in the blue and white tradition. It was, however, a luxury afforded only by the upper classes – most people still relied on the tin tub set up in the kitchen in front of the fire. Things continued like this until well into the twentieth century when the bathroom became an intrinsic room in most households. New houses built after the First World War were built with bathrooms included; ones built prior to this turned over an upstairs room for the purpose, so you can expect to find bathrooms in a variety of shapes and sizes – from a transformed bedroom with an open grate and mantelpiece, to a small box room turned into the most practical tiny bathroom. This offers tremendous potential as the room may have features which you want to enhance and use as a main focus. And, of course, blue and white are still predominant colour choices for bathrooms.

ABOVE *Crisp and fresh, only a few splashes of colour are needed to brighten this small bathroom.*

LEFT *Royal blue and white decor and geometric shapes give this small bathroom a practical quality.*

RIGHT *Bathrooms created from other rooms in old houses often contain interesting features which can be capitalized on.*

GILDED FISH

*Keep your bathroom oils and potions in a decorative bottle,
making good use of old wine bottles or kitchen jars*

1 First use a base coat which will give your bottle a rough surface to work on. A ceramic paint will work well for this purpose. Look for an opaque finish. Paint on the main colour using as many coats as necessary to cover it completely.

2 With your finger tip apply the gold paint in order to accentuate features. Use a dead matt varnish to seal the bottle so that it is suitable for use in the bathroom.

Antique fittings and warm tones make even a small bathroom seem interesting and welcoming.

There are three main elements which need to be accommodated when planning your bathroom – a bath or shower, basin and toilet. The range of fittings currently available allows you plenty of freedom to create original combinations. You could have cast iron, steel or acrylic for your bath. Cast iron and steel baths are sturdy and will last a lifetime. Acrylic baths are cheaper but don't wear well and scratch easily. As well as the choice of material for your bath you now have variety in shape and size. Fitted elements were once considered the ultimate luxury. Nowadays, although fitted bathrooms are still extremely sought after, the old styling of single pieces – such as freestanding cast iron baths with claw feet reminiscent of the traditional designs used when bathrooms first became popular – is once again fashionable. You don't have to worry if your room is an unusual shape: with the choice of corner baths, half-size baths and standing baths – popular throughout Europe – you'll find exactly what you're looking for. With standpipes coming out of the floor you can house your bath in the middle of the room, making it the central feature, or raise it and use a step up. Sunken baths are also fashionable or, for the ultimate in bathroom relaxation, you could invest in a whirlpool or spa. It is said that women prefer to bath, wallowing in a hot tub scented with oils and bubbles, luxuriating in the experience, whereas men prefer the fast, easy option of a refreshing shower. Over the last ten years developments in the quality and performance of showers have created a wide variety of shower options. You can have shower jets for all occasions – power jet, champagne or massage. Tiled shower cubicles provide the perfect setting for experimenting with your decoration, using a mix of extravagant tiles from top to bottom.

During the 1970s coloured bathroom suites were fashionable. Strong, deep colours such as avocado, brown, purple, teal and navy could be found everywhere. 1990s' fashion harps back to a much more traditional style. Bathroom manufacturers are experiencing a demand for Victorian-type white enamel suites. This is excellent news if you're considering decorating in blue and white. The Victorians, and later the Edwardians, loved this combination. White bathroom suites were enhanced with blue and white printed jugs and bowls standing by the tub and printed tiles as splashbacks. Ceramic handles, doorplates and light pulls echoed the colours with tiny blue and white floral designs synonymous with the traditional bathroom.

This dramatic mosaic with its Greek key border is reminiscent of the original Greek and Roman baths.

GLASS-PAINTED MIRROR

Discover how easy glass painting can be by making yourself this simple bathroom mirror

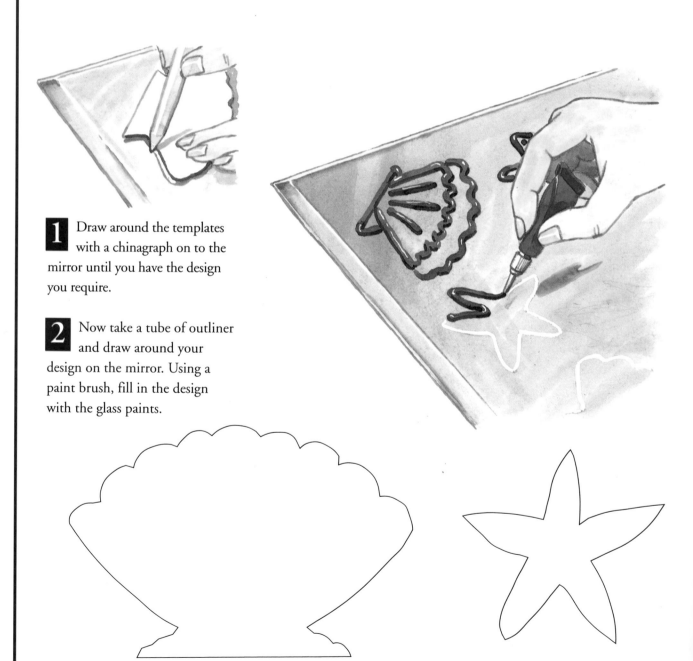

1 Draw around the templates with a chinagraph on to the mirror until you have the design you require.

2 Now take a tube of outliner and draw around your design on the mirror. Using a paint brush, fill in the design with the glass paints.

There are hundreds of different styles of tile to choose from, or you could design one yourself.

Tiled surfaces are ideal to decorate. A neat, white-tiled room is a magnet for the keen stenciller. Stencilling is an age-old technique commonly used for decorating walls and papers before the development of refined printing techniques. In Sweden it was widely used for all-over wall decoration, and nowadays it is fast becoming an extremely fashionable technique among home-decorating enthusiasts everywhere. With stencils you can repeat images easily without any fuss. You can create a frieze around the room or an all-over effect. Using each tile as a grid you can mix two or three different stencils to create a riot of visual effects. For a bathroom, small delicate designs work well. Fleur-de-lys or small floral sprigs are strong but simple designs which would bring impact and drama into the room. Use the fleur-de-lys as a frieze running around the room at waist height and mimic the design across the top of the room. Alternatively, use the floral sprigs randomly across the tiles, lifting the plainness of pure white. Some people like the idea of a more stark look so you could leave the tiles plain but alternate blue and white to look like a chequer board. The effect is simple but striking – reminiscent of the Moorish style

commonly seen across Southern Europe. Geometric stencils will give a different look altogether. With a single image – a triangle or square – you can create truly extraordinary effects. With two tones of blue work squares around the room or use them to frame a door or mirror or to define the top of a shelf. Create a Greek key stencil and give the room a Mediterranean feel. Sponging too is an effective technique on tiles. Simple shapes can be daubed across them to add texture and interest.

Paints, vinyls and wallpapers

You can add impact to your walls by using a variety of paint techniques. A blue and white theme lends itself to all manner of visual effects. You shouldn't be put off trying them, because most are relatively easy with a little practice and often it's the medium you use which creates the look – the only skill required is to master that medium and discover how it works best. Colour washing is an ideal finish for a bathroom: you paint one colour over another so that the base colour still shows through. Use white as your base coat with blue as the wash and the finish will be textured and translucent, giving the room a naive country feel. Without the dense colour of a flat tone you can use strong coloured washes which will be softened by the paler base coat. Use a water-based emulsion diluted with water. (Test different consistencies until you have a colour with which you are happy and make a note of the dilution so you can recreate the colour should you need to mix more.) Paint your base coat. When it's dry ensure that all dirt and dust have been wiped from the surface. Dilute your emulsion colour and mix it thoroughly. Apply the paint to the wall using random brush strokes – it's important that the strokes move in all directions and that there is no definite flow. Work in small areas, crossing the strokes over each other. Then use a dry brush to blur the effect and keep building colour until you have the look you're after. For colour washing wood the application is slightly different. Paint your diluted emulsion following the grain of the wood and then use a cloth to wipe away the paint. Repeat with the colour until you have the depth of tone you require. You can protect the paintwork when dry with a matt varnish. If you don't fancy painting the walls you could always wallpaper them. There are many bathroom vinyls available, some mimicking paint techniques, others recreating tiled effects. Pre-pasted papers are easy to apply so don't think wallpapering is a chore. The sturdy vinyl papers are easy to handle and, once you have matched patterns, are straightforward to hang.

Regency stripes give this bathroom a sense of formality and elegance.

FLEUR-DE-LYS TILE

Stencil a popular design with sponging on top

1 Make your stencil by tracing the design on the right on to stencil acetate. Cut out the stencil and fix it to your tile using a tacky mount spray.

2 Stipple through the stencil with your main colour. Lift the stencil and repeat on your next tile.

3 Use a paler colour lightly loaded on a sponge to add a speckled texture to the alternating tiles.

Panelling and insets

If you decide upon a fitted bathroom and want to create visual impact with your units consider using panelling and insets. Using these combinations can unify a room, carrying through a theme between all the units. Insets can also be a practical way of covering pipes and housing bowls and cisterns. Wood-panelled bath fronts and wood-stained cabinets are ideal for applied decoration. Use colour washing or a stain before adding the design. There are numerous techniques you could use to apply detail. The most obvious

Create unusual decorative effects in your bathroom with your choice of accessories.

and foolproof is stencilling. Others to try include freestyle painting, decorative folk art and découpage.

Modern additions

Blue and white rooms are so simple and refreshing it makes accessorizing easy. Once your fittings are in place and you've decided upon the theme for decoration, you can begin to personalize your bathroom. Wandering around the shops will fill you with inspiration. There is such a wide choice of decorative items available in the stores today. People have an innate desire to prettify and traders are meeting the demand by filling their shelves with colourful trinkets to display in your home. With some imagination you could pretend you made them yourself but this is the way of the fainthearted – making and decorating for yourself is actually good fun and far more satisfying than simply buying something made by somebody else. Do use the shops for inspiration, though; some of the ideas you'll see are quite original.

Ideas

Bathrooms lend themselves beautifully to decorative additions. Shelves and cupboards mean there are surfaces to be filled. The walls and floor you can decorate, but outside of that it's the surfaces which can give additional detail. If you have a bathroom which was once a bedroom you may have a fireplace with a mantel, so tile the surround with blue and white delft-type tiles and make a feature of the fire. Complement the tiles by displaying deep blue medicine jars on the shelf filled with your favourite oils and bath salts. In a blue and white bathroom you could simply choose a plain white shower curtain. If you'd like to lift it, however, why not use fabric paints to add bold lino prints or mirror the design of a frieze along the top of the curtain? Alternatively paint the colour on to a leaf and use it as a printing block. By cleverly placing the prints you can create the effect of a fall of colour culminating in a pool of leaves at the bottom of the curtain. Use your towels decoratively by carrying through the theme of the room. Buy plain towels with an insert panel which can be embroidered, then create your own design for the towels by using graph paper to draw out a picture. You can trace over any image you like and turn it into an embroidery design. Simple ideas often work best, especially in a room with a single colour theme, so you don't have to be the ultimate artist – just somebody with a little imagination and the commitment to learn a couple of easy embroidery stitches. You can echo your embroidery design with a stencil border. Shells are simple shapes which would work well and could be translated in both mediums. With blue's close association to sun, sea and sand shells provide an ideal design source.

Collect pictures cut out from magazines for ideas. Nobody is expected to create without inspiration; even the best designers rely on any number of sources for ideas. Look through art books to see how earlier cultures used design and colour, and experiment: use their ideas mixed with your own for original results.

You don't have to make everything. Having looked through books and magazines and seen what's available in the stores, you should by now have a crystal clear picture of how you'd like your bathroom to look and the finishing touches can be added with a little help from ready-made sources. Essentials, such as soap and bath oils, can all add to the overall picture of your room. Look for coloured soaps and oils and display them in a blue and white bowl. Paint a metal plant holder, place a bowl or pot inside it and use it to store creams and bottles. Green and blue work well together, even though the saying suggests 'blue and green should never be seen'. An array of greenery in your bathroom will add contrast and plants thrive in the humid environment as long as there is natural light. Look for interesting pots and planters to echo your colour theme.

Rich, fresh and exciting: colour works so well when combined with a little forethought.

TOWEL AND FLANNEL SET

*Counted thread cross stitch designs worked on special
towels and flannels bought from craft shops – the strip
of aida-band at each end is intended for embroidery.*

1 Wash and iron the towel
and flannel to minimize
further shrinkage or colour
bleeding. The design is worked
on the narrow strip of aida-band.
Following the chart below, count
the number of threads from the
edge of the aida-band to find the
centre of the design, and mark
this point with a tacking stitch.

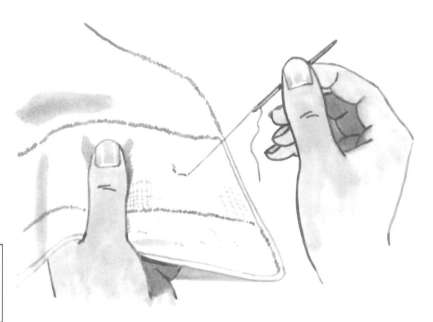

Use stranded cotton in two threads
- ● light blue thread
- ● dark blue thread
- ● black backstitch thread

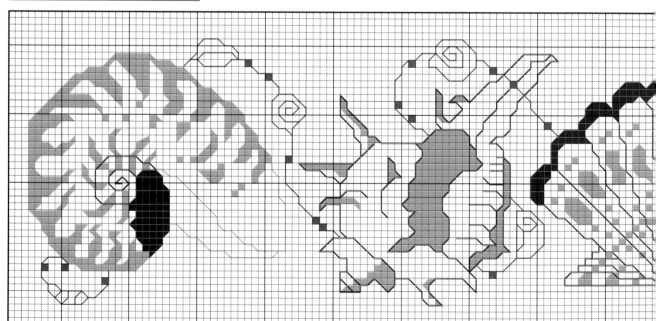

2 The design uses three colours. The filled in squares on the chart represent cross stitches, while the diagonal lines are back stitch. Follow the chart, counting as you go, and work from the centre towards the outside.

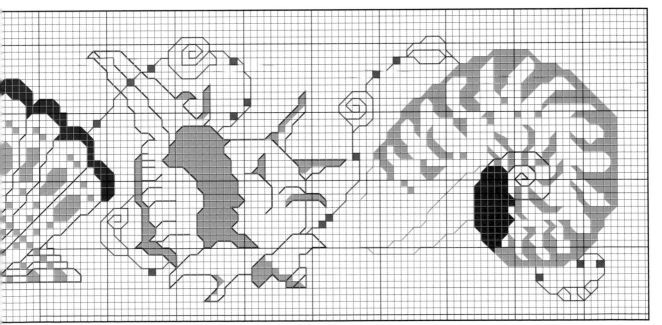

BEDROOMS

ABOVE *A child's room may also double as a playroom, and should therefore be as cheerful as possible.*

There's never been a place quite so perfect as the room in which you sleep. Shutting the world out means it's the most private place and it can be decorated to please oneself as it doesn't have to be shown to others. It's important that it's comfortable and it's important that it's functional, but beyond that it's a place where you can pander to your whims and fantasies. It can exist in many forms: elegant master rooms, fresh guest rooms or cheerful children's rooms. You can be warm and fluffy or cool and reserved. Monotone colours worked with strong Japanese inspirations could be as appealing as a four-poster bed wrapped with chiffon drapes. A country room could be warmed with pine and terracotta, a big room with lashings of deep blue and mahogany. All you need to consider is who the room is for. If you share a room with husband, partner, brother or sister you may find compromises are necessary, especially when a man and a woman share as their tastes can be so very different. Don't expect a man to live happily with candy pink silks. Nor is it practical to fill a child's bedroom with expensive ornaments. Once you have the right room for the right person, you can create a bedroom that's unique.

RIGHT *Use fabric with imagination as drapes or as a hanging behind the bedhead. Add crisp white cushions and sheets.*

LEFT Duotones are dramatic and add depth to small spaces.

RIGHT Your bedroom, unlike other rooms in the house, is a private haven, so you can feel free to fill it with your favourite colours and personal possessions.

Bedrooms and colour

Blue is an appropriate colour for a bedroom. With the choice of tones and hues available it is neither predominantly male nor female and it's a practical colour for walls, furnishings and woodwork because it's so easy to live with. There's an age-old association of women with florals and pastel colours and men with strong, dark colours and simple furnishings. If this is the problem, then blue can be an absolute boon. It's a universal colour which, when used with appropriate tones and combinations, will satisfy everyone.

The focal piece of furniture in a bedroom has to be the bed and with so many styles available this in itself can give the theme for the rest of the furnishings. You could choose pine, a dark wood, a steel frame, brass, divan or a futon, with each of these choices having unique characteristics and all having a very different look. Each will recreate a period or style which you can build upon to create your desired effect. Bedding, soft furnishings and furniture will complete the overall picture. The bedroom should be relaxing, with colours that calm and help you to unwind. Colours which can do this are blues, greens, pastels and earth tones. Primaries tend to grate. A profusion of white can look and feel clinical, unless it's worked in combination with warmer, more welcoming tones. A child's room can take bright colours because children need the inspiration and stimulation of something cheery. Spots, stripes, mobiles, pictures and toys all go to make a child's room exciting. A master bedroom would have to be approached another way as the needs of the occupants are different.

COLOUR WASHED DRESSER

*Soft blues rubbed back to a gentle wash will look elegant
and atmospheric in your bedroom. Add some stencilling
to give more elaborate detail*

1 Apply two coats of knotting solution around the knots. When dry, apply a cloudy blue wash over each knot (fig.1), then apply some shellac to keep the look of the grain.

2 When dry, apply cobalt plus white emulsion, a section at a time. When tacky, drag off a little with a clean damp cloth (fig.2). Then apply the second colour of blue.

3 Take some blue-grey acrylic paint on an almost dry 2 inch brush and drag it scratchily through the grain. Next apply a quick-drying acrylic water-based varnish with some blue-grey water-based acrylic added. To age, rub across the grain with a damp lint-free cloth before the varnish is fully dry. Rub down with fine wire wool, then stencil the piece. Rub over the stencil with wire wool to soften (fig.3). Use dark beeswax and fine wire wool to finish.

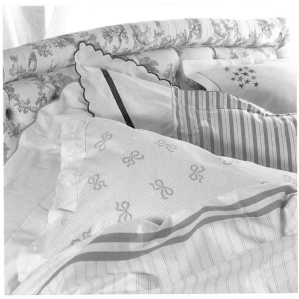

Bold gingham checks combined with crisp white linen make a room feel fresh.

Pastel blues and soft whites will give your bedding a romantic elegance.

Ask yourself, then, various questions before you start. Who is the room for? Apart from sleeping, what will it be used for? It's natural that there should be storage for clothes and bedding, but what personal effects need to be accommodated within the room? Most bedrooms will have a bed, a chest of drawers, a wardrobe and a mirror. Others may vary slightly, with shelving instead of drawers or a rail instead of a wardrobe, but the essentials tend to be pivotal in every bedroom with the personal touches and decorative finishes making the room unique. Do you want the furniture to coordinate with the bed or do you want the pieces to stand separately? Do you want a country feel or a period feel or would you prefer a modern looking room with bold colour and furnishings?

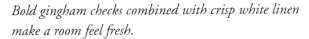

LEFT *Make the most of a small room by coordinating all the details.*

Have you discussed your ideas with your partner, more importantly, and have you reached a conclusion on which you both agree? There have been instances recorded where one partner has not been able to sleep because the bedroom made them feel uncomfortable rather than relaxed and calm.

Blue is a naturally calming colour, although in its pure tones it can be a cold colour. With five per cent black or five per cent red added to the colour palette it immediately warms. Lighting, too, will change the mood of a room. Have soft lighting in a bedroom, reflecting off the walls, to give the room additional warmth. Rooms with a lot of natural light can take cool colours without appearing cold. Use a burnt orange for accents, as it sits exactly opposite blue on the colour wheel and works beautifully to lift colours in a blue room. Your soft furnishings will also lift the room and the ideal way of doing this is with your bedding.

LEFKARA CUSHION

*Use Cypriot Lefkara work to create a romantic bedroom
cushion with drawn thread and geometric embroidery.*

1 You need an 18 inch
square of 28 count linen
and a ball of crochet cotton.
The design comprises 16
motifs, each in a 3 inch square
bordered by drawn thread
embroidery.

To create the squares,
measure down from the top of
the fabric 1 inch and withdraw
the thread below. Leave three
threads and withdraw the next.
Measure down 3 inches and
repeat this sequence until you
have done it four times in all.
Turn the fabric and repeat
along the adjacent side. This
will give you 16 squares.

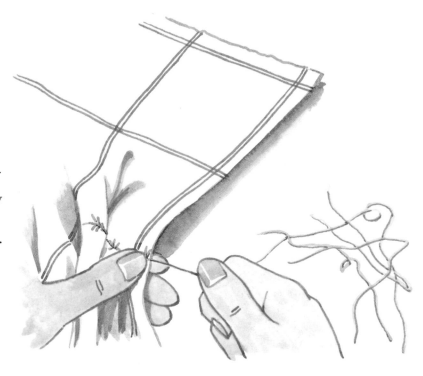

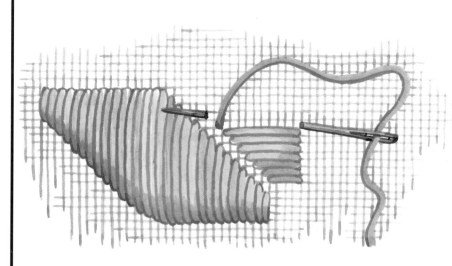

2 Following the
instructions opposite,
start stitching the border,
always working over the three
undrawn threads. Then work
the motifs in satin stitch
(fig.2), following the chart
overleaf. Start at the centre of
each motif, and make the
stitches between the bold
black lines.

3 To make up the cushion cut a 4 inch wide strip of material 1 ½ times the length of the outside edge of your embroidered linen. Fold the strip in half lengthways and press. Run a gathering thread ½ inch in from the raw edge and pull up to fit the outside edge of the linen. With the frill facing in, stitch it to the right side of the linen. Cut your backing fabric to the same size as the linen. Place the backing on top of it, right sides together, and sew around the edges, leaving a gap for turning. Turn; insert a pad. Finish by slipstitching.

Border instructions Work from the chart over the three vertical undrawn threads and across the three horizontal threads. Continue working this way until the border is finished. Start by bringing your needle up at 1.

1			2
4			3
6			5
8			7
10			9
12			11
			13

1 - 2 - 1
1 - 2 - 3
3 - 2 - 4
4 - 1 - 4
4 - 3 - 4
4 - 3 - 5
5 - 3 - 6
6 - 4 - 6
6 - 5 - 6
6 - 5 - 7
7 - 6 - 8
8 - 6 - 8
8 - 7 - 8
8 - 7 - 9
and
continue

Ideas

Bedding offers an ideal opportunity to revel in the potential of traditional techniques such as embroidery and cutwork. Cutwork, or open work, is particularly suitable. Usually worked on linen or an even weave fabric, areas of the ground fabric are withdrawn from the weave. A buttonhole stitch is used to bind the edges and decorative satin stitch and needle weaving used to fill the holes. The results can be extremely delicate and beautiful. This type of work has been very popular on peasant embroidery throughout the world since the Middle Ages. As the technique has evolved the standard of workmanship has become exquisite. In Italy, Richelieu and Venetian ladder work are two particularly fine examples of cutwork embroidery where strips of fabric were decoratively joined together with laddering or faggoting. Cutwork was often worked in white threads on a white foundation fabric, but as it

A checked design looks good on a headboard: mark with a pencil and ruler, then use acrylic paints.

evolved and became popular in a spread of countries each adopted its own unique way of interpreting the style. In Cyprus, traditional Lefkara embroidery was worked on an oatmeal linen with earth colour threads. For Hardanger, a Norwegian cutwork, a single colour thread would be worked on a contrasting background, and *broderie anglaise* – which became popular in the eighteenth century – was always worked white on white. These traditional embroidery techniques were used for household textiles: for decorating tablecloths, shelf edging and pillows, and for edging sheets. The patterns were often geometric or stylized, worked in blocks and stars or tiny florals. Italian Richelieu embroidery, however, incorporated figurative and floral designs, making it more finely detailed and lace-like than the naive peasant crafts of elsewhere.

Instructions for charts opposite

Chart 1 Leave the inside squares blank.

Chart 2 Stitch only around the rectangles, leaving the insides blank.

Chart 3 Leave the middle square blank

Chart 4 Stitch the squares only.

Chart 5 Leave the inside rectangles blank.

Chart 6 Stitch the irregular shapes, leaving the boxes blank.

Enlarge charts to 150% for ease of working.

PATCHWORK QUILT

*Use basic patchwork technique to create a New England
Amish style quilt*

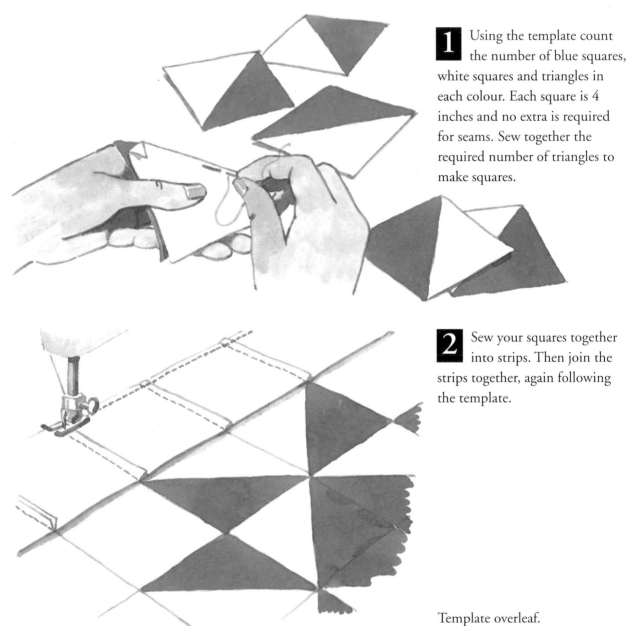

1 Using the template count the number of blue squares, white squares and triangles in each colour. Each square is 4 inches and no extra is required for seams. Sew together the required number of triangles to make squares.

2 Sew your squares together into strips. Then join the strips together, again following the template.

Template overleaf.

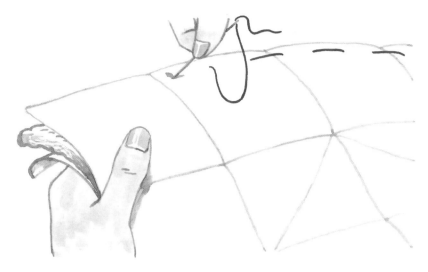

3 Cut the 2oz wadding and backing fabric the same size as your finished quilt. Tack the top, wadding and backing fabric together, then stitch binding around the edges, finishing on the wrong side. Using a running stitch, quilt through all the layers around each pattern to finish.

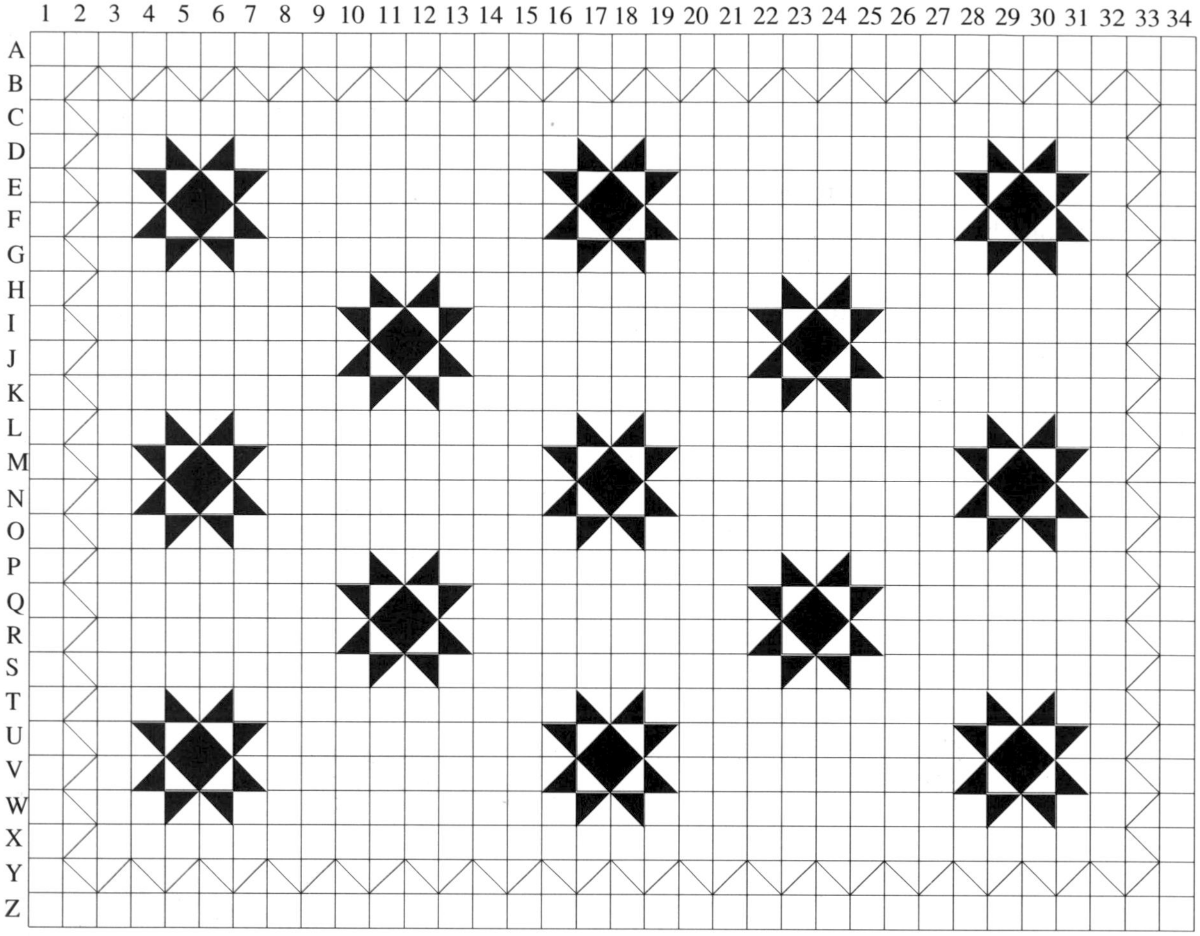
1 2 3 4 5 6 7 8 9 10 11 12 13 14 15 16 17 18 19 20 21 22 23 24 25 26 27 28 29 30 31 32 33 34
A B C D E F G H I J K L M N O P Q R S T U V W X Y Z

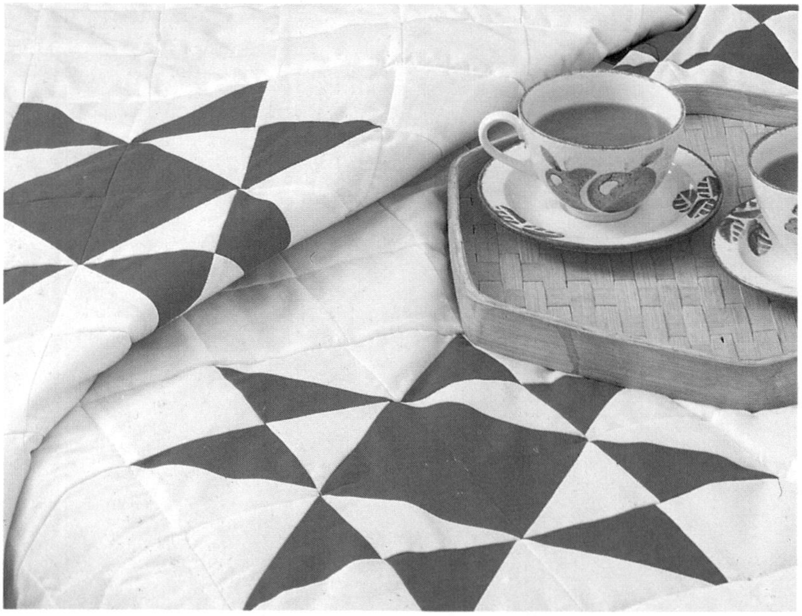

Follow the layout for the quilt, working it column by column. Match your squares and triangles to those shown above. The zigzag around the edge is a possible starting point for your quilting. Use a machine, or hand stitch. Alternatively, you could quilt around each of the motifs or along blocks of vertical or horizontal columns.

Quilting and patchwork are also ideal needle crafts to use in the bedroom. Traditional Amish quilts, popularized by the North American Amish settlers, would lend themselves beautifully to a blue and white bedroom. The style uses strong blocks of colour worked into a plain background, often with the pattern appliquéd over a background fabric – geometrics and stylized florals were the preferred ornamentation with a raised, textured effect achieved by quilting through layers filled with wadding. Patchwork quilts are made from scraps and oddments of fabric which are stitched together to create pattern. Again the pattern types are traditional and colour is used in a variety of tones to create stunning effects. The finish differs depending how the colours are sewn together. A night and day quilt, for instance, is identified by the use of light colour fabrics working against dark, to give a shadowed effect. The quilts are made with pieces of tiny print fabrics. These small prints were popularized in America but with the growing interest in patchwork can now be found in many specialist stitch shops.

A combination of checks, stars and stripes and a simple antique bed gives this room an early American look.

LEFT *A mixture of turquoise, sky blue and teal make a brilliant impact on this day bed converted from a traditional French iron bedstead.*

RIGHT *Soft drapes and elegant furnishings create a feeling of decadent luxury.*

If you'd rather try something more modern you could use appliqué to make your own, more contemporary quilt, but don't totally disregard the influence of American quilts. The Americans have a history of making the most beautiful covers and have many years of expert experience behind them, with their tried and tested techniques. Use their designs as inspiration to see what's possible. You'll be surprised at the number of different effects that can be achieved.

If you've never tried embroidery, don't be put off. During the Middle Ages it was considered an honourable craft practised by both men and women. During the seventeenth and eighteenth centuries embroidery was a pastime almost purely reserved for the upper classes – in fact, Louis XV of France was considered an extremely fine embroiderer. In terms of kudos,

therefore, it's something you really should try. You should also try it for the sake of enjoyment. It's probably best to start working with a single colour thread. You can introduce yourself slowly to the potential of the craft and as you master working with a single colour you can move on, add more colours and eventually try some of the many different types of work. The choice is phenomenal, ranging from needlepoint to crewel work. Nowadays embroidery tends to be used as an art medium for creating pictures. It's extremely expensive and so non-commercial to produce hand-decorated furnishings for sale. Mass production techniques allow for cheaper, more affordable imitations, but if you want the real thing, your only option is to do it yourself. It's a pleasurable pastime which would certainly guarantee that the furnishings in your bedroom are completely unique.

TECHNIQUES AND EQUIPMENT

Colour and how to use it

The human eye can recognize over ten million different colours. It's no wonder therefore that we may have difficulty choosing a specific shade. You need to know how colour works and the effects which can be achieved by each colour's use. Firstly there are primary colours: pure red, pure yellow and pure blue. These true colours cannot be made by mixing together any others. They can, however, be mixed with other colours to make an infinite spectrum of tones. Secondary colours – orange, green and violet – can be made by mixing equal amounts of two primaries. The colours which contrast most, but still work together, sit on opposite sides of the colour wheel: blue and orange, for example. Harmonious colours, such as blue and green, lie next to each other on the wheel; their base colour is the same. Shades can be created by adding a small amount of a second colour, more commonly black or white. You can make subtle changes to a shade by adding a touch of blue, red or yellow.

Blue is a cool colour, ideal if you want to create a cool, calm atmosphere. Cool colours tend to make rooms look bigger than they actually are. In a dark room they may have the

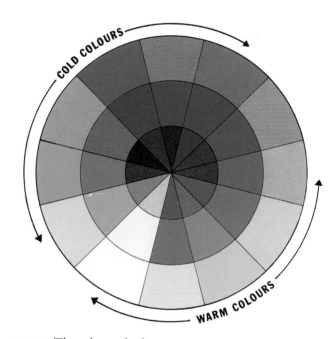

ABOVE *The colour wheel.*

RIGHT *Blue is a versatile colour with which you can achieve both bold and subdued effects.*

effect of making the room seem austere. A light room can take cool colours without appearing cold and this is perhaps one of the reasons why blue is used so extensively in Mediterranean climates. Add yellow to blue to give it warmth. For a softer look use pastel blues. Pastels work well with other tones of pastel because they all contain a high concentration of white.

Painting furniture

Paint brushes

Choosing a brush is not always easy as there is such a wide choice available. There are, however, certain types of brushes which work best for specific techniques and this is worth considering if you want to try your hand at decorative painting.

Stencil brushes – Made from hard-wearing bristle, these are round, coarse, stubby brushes with a flat head, ideal for stippling through a stencil.

Standard decorating brushes – In a range of sizes, these are available from any decorating shop. The head may be bristle or synthetic. They are used for applying gloss or emulsion paint or glaze.

Liners – These are standard art brushes used for creating fine lines and detail. The hairs on the brush are proportionally longer than those on a watercolour brush.

Use your imagination and experiment to discover a wealth of decorative craft techniques.

Flats – Flat brushes with square ends which are used to produce wide, thin detail.

Dusting brushes – These brushes are used to remove dust from a surface before painting. They are also used as stipplers or to soften hard paint lines.

Stippling brushes – Used in the same way as the dusting brushes, these stipple a surface or soften hard paint lines.

Sponges – There are two types of sponges: natural and synthetic. The natural sponge is more expensive but a sponged finish using one is more effective than a finish achieved with a synthetic sponge.

With paints, dyes and brushes the creative possibilities are endless.

Paints, varnishes and glazes

There are two main types of paints, water-based and oil- or solvent- based. You have to be careful which one you use as they are not both suitable for all effects.

Water-based

Emulsion – An effective wall covering which comes in a range of colours and is relatively inexpensive. Emulsion can be diluted for colour washing.

Milk paint – This gives a chalky finish. The powder can be diluted for colour washing. Milk paint is not waterproof, so should be sealed after painting.

Lime wash – This provides a matt, reflective finish which can be tinted to any colour.

Pigment wash – A powdery finish, again suitable for colour washing when diluted.

Gouache – This is used for painting designs on to a surface or for colouring water-based tints.

Acrylics – These are used for tinting water-based paints and glazes as well as for working stencil designs.

Emulsion glaze – As it provides a transparent glaze which can be tinted to a range of fast-drying colours this kind of paint is used for decorative effects.

Oil-based

Gloss – A high shine paint used almost exclusively as a top coat for woodwork. It's hard-wearing, readily available and comes in a wide range of colours.

Eggshell – It has a softer sheen than a gloss, but is still hard-wearing so is used mainly as a top coat for woodwork. You can also buy a water-based eggshell. It works well as a ground for decorative paint effects.

Satin wood – A medium shine gloss, used to cover woodwork. Again this can be bought in as water-based.

Artist's oil colour – Use this for tinting oil-based paints, and glazes.

Transparent oil glaze – Used for decorative effects, this provides a transparent glaze which can be tinted to a range of colours.

Ceramics

Clays

Most clays are worked and then fired in a kiln to fuse the finished shape. The clays used in this book are self-hardening new clays. They do not need firing, so the projects are easily achievable at home. The clay has been mixed with nylon. Once it has been worked the nylon hardens to produce a durable, water resistant vessel. Mixed with water the wet clay is malleable and can be moulded into any shape you require. Simply leave the finished piece to dry out.

Paints

Paint manufacturers are making the art of ceramic painting available for all. As well as producing pigments which need firing they have produced a range of ceramic paints which you simply paint on to your finished pot, bowl or plate and leave to dry. They come in a range of vibrant colours which retain their density over time. Although the colours are durable they will not stand up to constant washing. They are ideal for decorative effects. Acrylic paints also work well on ceramics; they are easy to use and have a vast colour range. The opaque colours sit on the surface, so acrylics are ideal for wares with a porous body.

Paint techniques

Resists

You can use resists to create a range of intriguing effects. A resist is simply a medium which will reject dye, so any area covered with a resist will remain the same as the base colour once additional dye is added over the exposed areas.

For instance, you can achieve some delicate effects by painting with wax. First melt the wax and then use it as you would paint. After the initial dyeing you can add wax and dye again. The second application will pick up the colour the fabric has just been dyed. When you're happy with the effect fix the dyes and wash – or iron in the case of wax – the resist out of the fabric. Popular resists are wax, starch pastes such as flour and water and synthetic guttas.

Dyes

If you're printing on fabric you will need a different dyeing medium than you would for working on wood and walls. While you can stencil with acrylics on walls, this would not fix on fabric. Look for paints or creams specifically designed for fabrics. For ease of use within the home look for heat-fixed dyes. Your choices will be either heat-fixed or steam-fixed. Steam-fixed dyes are fine, but if you're dyeing a quantity of fabric you'll need a big steam bath. Heat-fixing can be done with an iron.

Fabrics

Types and effects

If you're using fabric for household furnishings you need to consider what the finished item will be used for. Will it be used often? Is it something that will be displayed? Will there be a lot of light on it? Will it be washed often? Does the material need to be hard-wearing? Will you be colouring or dyeing the fabric? These are all primary considerations.

Cotton – This is a fabric widely used for furnishings. It comes in a variety of weights and textures so is suitable for crisp table linen, curtains and cushions. Drills and calicos are hard-wearing and dye easily. As it is a natural fibre cotton has a tendency to shrink. It's important to wash it before making up.

125

Silk – Considered to be a luxurious fibre, silk is not particularly hard-wearing but is excellent for dyeing. The fabric has a natural lustre and, when painted, the colours pick this up. Colours worked on damp silk bleed and mix, producing unique effects. For smaller household items silk looks perfect, but don't expect it to wear well. Wash it first to counteract any shrinkage.

Linen – A firm, crisp fabric, linen does not wash too well and creases badly. It is ideal for embroidery because the definite, loose weave is easy to stitch on.

Synthetic fabrics – Fabrics such as polyester are durable and easy to care for. They imitate many natural fabrics but with a slight sheen. They don't, however, take dye as well as natural fabrics.

All fabrics react to excessive light: too much and the fibres will weaken and colours fade.

Iron-on interfacing

To make appliqué easy use a double-sided iron-on fusible interfacing. First iron it to your motifs, then peel off the backing and iron it in place on the ground fabric. You can then stitch around the motifs. Using this interfacing takes the strain out of appliqué, making it quicker and helping to eliminate any mistakes.

Threads

If you are using natural fabrics choose a mercerized cotton thread. This is stronger than a normal sewing thread and will stand up to everyday use. On synthetics use a synthetic thread. For outlining appliqué by machine use

a bold machine thread for the top stitching. If your machine will not take the bulk of a thicker thread, stick with a mercerized cotton and use a closely worked satin stitch or zigzag. If you're attaching motifs by hand, use buttonhole stitch with two strands of cotton embroidery thread.

Fire proofing

If you're using fabrics for home furnishings look for ones which have been treated with a fire retardant. If the fabric you want has not been treated, back it with a fire resistant lining which can be bought quite cheaply from fabric shops.

Embroidery

Needles

Needles used for needlepoint are blunt with a large eye. They are called tapestry needles. The blunt end slips easily through the holes in the canvas and the yarn can be threaded easily through the eye. Any needle between sizes 18 to 26 is ideal for needlepoint and cross stitch projects. (The higher the number the finer the needle.) For freestyle embroidery you need a sharper needle.

Fabrics

Canvas – Originally derived from hemp, canvas is a coarse yet versatile medium which is ideal for needlepoint. The canvas is woven with either an even weave single or double thread. An even weave is suitable for all needlepoint projects although it is prone to distort when handled. The double thread is stronger as pairs

Different weights and textures of fabrics require different sewing materials and methods.

of threads are woven together to form a more rigid construction. The weave can also be split, allowing you to work half stitches and create fine detail within your design.

Linen – Ideal for embroidery, the even weave of the fibres in linen can be worked with ease and for cutwork the fibres pull with no problem.

The difference between canvases is determined by the number of holes per inch. The greater the number of holes per inch the finer the design. A large count can be fiddly to work and the design may take longer to grow than it would if you were working on a smaller gauge. The most frequently used canvases are between 10 and 16 holes to the inch.

Threads

Needlepoint projects tend to be worked in tapestry yarn. A tapestry yarn is generally 100% wool. It does not stretch like a knitting yarn and is stronger and harder-wearing. You can split the strands to work in one, two, three or four strands as the pattern suggests. For cross stitch and other counted thread embroidery stranded cottons are most commonly used. The threads are fine and lustrous and can be split for differing densities of colour. You can work out the amount of thread you will need by measuring off a length of yarn and working a test section of your canvas until you run out of thread. Work out how many stitches you'll need in each colour by counting the blocks on the chart. Give yourself a 20% margin for mistakes and starting and finishing.

INDEX

aida-band 100–1
American craft work 16, 25, 28, 32, 40, 45, 64, 117–18
Amish style 117
apothecary blue 45
appliqué 117–18, 126
Art Deco style 15, 72
Art Nouveau style 15
Arts and Crafts movement 14–15, 65

basket weave effect 68
bathrooms 84–101
bedrooms 102–19
        child's 102, 103
blind, potato printed 30
block printing 81, 99
bottles, painted 88–9
bowls, decorated 26–7
box lids, découpage 50–1
Bristol glass 45
broderie anglaise 113
brushes, paint 123

candlestick, verdigris 62–3
ceramics 10, 13–14, 16, 40–1, 48–9, 72, 74–7, 80–1, 99, 125
        see also tiles
Chinese wares 10, 12, 13, 80
chinoiserie 60
chintzes 60
cobalt 10, 13, 40, 45, 77, 80
coffee table, clouded 82–3
colour washing 94–5, 98, 106–8
colour wheel 120
combing 68
cross stitch 100–1, 127
Cubist style 15
curtains
        café 25
        resist 66–7
        shower 99
        tiebacks for 46–7
cushions 78–9, 81, 110–12
cutwork 113
cylinder printing 61
Cypriot embroidery 113

de Morgan, William 15
découpage 49–51, 98
Delft, delft ware 13
dining rooms 34–51
dining table 36
distressing furniture 22, 32
dragging 68

drawn thread work 110–12
dresser, colour washed 106–8
dyes 125

earthenware 13
Elizabeth I, Queen 84
embroidery 99, 100–1, 110–13, 118, 127

fabrics 125–6
        for embroidery 127
        for kitchens 25, 32
        printing 38–9, 60–1, 78, 81
Faenza 13
faience 13
fitted kitchens 20
fleur-de-lys designs 94, 96
flooring 72
folk art, decorative 98
Frijtom, Frederick van 13
furniture 72, 76, 78, 81, 82–3, 109

garden rooms 70–83
glass, glassware 33, 45, 48–9, 72, 92–3
glazes 72, 77
Great Exhibition (1851) 65

Hardanger work 113
Huguenots 61

ikat effect 46–7
indigo 9–10, 17
Industrial Revolution 14, 61
interfacing 126
Islamic style 80–1

jasperware 13

key pattern, Greek 80, 94
kitchens 18–24

lapis lazuli 10
Lefkara embroidery 110–13
lighting 109
lino prints 78, 99
living rooms 52–69

marbling 82–3
Mediterranean pottery 32, 80–1
mirror, painted 92–3
mood boards 59
Moorish art 24–5, 81, 94
Morris, William 14–15, 64–5

needlepoint 127

needles 127
neo-classicical style 40–1

paint effects, decorative 68, 88–9, 92–3, 94–5, 98, 125
paints 124–5
panelling 98
patchwork 114–17
picture mount, border for 42–4
pigments 9–10, 77, 80
pintados 60
plant pots 99
        painted 74–5
potato prints 16, 30, 38–9
pots see ceramics
Potsdam (ceramics) 45
Provençal style 16, 22, 28, 32
Prussian blue 10

quilting 114–19

ragging 68
resist technique 66–7, 72, 77, 125

showers 90
slip decoration 77, 81
sponges 123
sponging 26–7, 48, 68, 94, 96–7
Staffordshire ware 13
stained glass 72
stencilling 16–17, 32, 42–4, 48, 81, 94, 96–7, 98, 99, 106–8
Syrian earthenware 81

tablecloths 25, 38–9
techniques and equipment 120–7
threads 126–7
tie dyeing 17
tiles 59, 72, 81, 90, 94, 96–7, 98
Toiles de Jouy 61
towel and flannel set 100–1
towels 99
transfer printing 14, 40, 86

ultramarine 10

verdigris 10, 62–3

wallpapers 64–5, 95
Wedgwood 13, 40–1
whitewashing 20
Willow Pattern 60
woad 9
Worcester 13